# Advanced Reader Copy

**Thank you for reading our book. Please protect it.**

Please:

📚 Read an Advanced reader copy

📚 Write a short review 1-3 sentences to include int he book & promo material **(by Oct 25).**

\*\* Include your name & (credentials: role/title or book title).

📚 Thank you in advance.

Ideal early readers:

🤚 People of Jewish heritage

🤚 Historians & Immigrants

🤚 People currrious about ancestry

When we are done, your blurb will be on the first pages of the book (see the next pages). \*One of our blurbs will be on the back cover.

# Praise for Oy Vey, It's Always Something

As I read Jean's story, I felt every emotion she experienced. I cried with her through the painful moments, laughed at her adventures and antics, and shared in her joy during the happy times. In every chapter I felt the deep compassion and forgiveness that defined her spirit – this book both moved and inspired me. For anyone who loves genuine, heartfelt nonfiction and true stories of resilience, humor, and love, you'll give it five stars too.

— Laura Hepp

*Oy Vey, It's Always Something* is a journey of the soul — a reminder that every challenge conceals divine purpose. With warmth and insight, Jean reveals how faith, mindfulness, and perseverance illuminate even the darkest moments. She inspires all of us to seek the spark of holiness within all things and to live each day with joy, purpose, and connection to G-d.

— Rabbi Yakov Borenstein

I loved how *Oy Vey, It's Always Something* transported me back to the early 1900s so I could share in this Jewish immigrant family's world from beginning to end. They had an abundance of love and deep connections to their Jewish traditions and faith, and that's all that mattered. This book made me proud of the immigrant Jews who came to America to start a better life and at the same time continue to honor their Jewish traditions and values.

— Shira Rothman

I brought *Oy Vey, It's Always Something* with me on vacation. Once I started to read same, I could hardly put it down because I wanted to find out what was next, next, etc. My only disappointment came when I finished reading the book and there was no more! I would recommend Oy Vey to all who appreciate family warmth, sentimentality, and family history.

— Mortimer I. Gordon, BGEN USAF (RET)

# Oy Vey, It's Always Something

## A 20th-Century Jewish Memoir

### Second Edition

**Jean Issacson**

Foreword by
**Steven A. Schechter**

Original Copyright © 1998 by Jean Issacson

Printed and C&M Press

Denver, Colorado

Republished with permission 2025 by Steven A. Schechter

Red Thread Publishing LLC. 2025

Write to **info@redthreadbooks.com** if you are interested in publishing with Red Thread Publishing. Learn more about publications or foreign rights acquisitions of our catalog of books: www.redthreadbooks.com

Ebook ISBN: 979-8-89294-055-9

Paperback ISBN: 979-8-89294-053-5

Hardcover ISBN: 979-8-89294-054-2

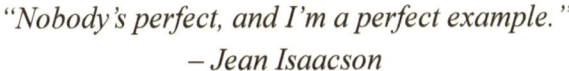

*"Nobody's perfect, and I'm a perfect example."*
*– Jean Isaacson*

# Epigraph

The anti-Semite: "All the troubles come from the Jews."
The Jew: "Absolutely, from the Jews and the bicycle riders."
The anti-Semite: "The bicycle riders, why the bicycle riders?"
The Jew: "Why the Jews?"

# In Appreciation
## From the Original

*My Mama and Papa who taught me well, and my brothers and sister who enriched my life.*
*My husband Irv who kept me laughing.*

*My daughter Candy for the love and encouragement that she has always given me.*
*My grandsons Steve and Ron, for asking for the family history, and the joy it gives me to leave this legacy.*
*My West Colfax Jewish neighbors who contributed to some of the stories in this book.*
*June Davis and Bev Cantlin who rescued the book from the waste basket when I was no longer physically able to complete it.*
*Dalyce Montgomery who proofread my book.*
*Dona Mandell who always takes something good and makes it special, created the cover and the illustrations.*

*Jean Isaacson*
*Denver, Colorado, USA*
*February 1998*

*Family Picture, 1922 Papa and Sam had suits from Sam's Bar Mitzvah and Izzy just got a suit for his Bar Mitzvah, so Mama said, "Now was the time for a picture!"*

# Contents

# Foreword
## Steven A. Schechter

בייה

When talking to my grandmother as a small child, I couldn't say grandma, so I called her Bam. My grandfather Irv felt he was too young for us to call him Grandpa, so we called him Papa. My brother Ron and I couldn't wait to stay at Bam and Papa's every Friday night after school. Every weekend we were  busy helping Bam without knowing she was keeping us out of the way. When doing laundry, my brother Ron and I would take turns ironing the rags as they came out of the dryer. It took a year before she plugged the iron in.

When she was busy getting the kitchen ready for *Shabbat*, lunch would frequently have mashed potatoes. Her trick here was teaching us how to make balls of mashed potatoes in our hands and then suck them out from the circle our little fists made with our index fingers and our thumbs. We were occupied playing with our food long enough for her to prepare *Shabbat* dinner.

Sometimes we got story time before naps. One time, she let us pick a story to read. We asked her to read one that our mom would read, Mother Goose's "The Three Little Kittens:"

The three little kittens, they lost their mittens,

And they began to cry.

"Oh, mother dear, we sadly fear,

That we have lost our mittens."

"What! Lost your mittens, you naughty kittens!

Then you shall have no pie."

*"What, no pie!"* Bam would yell at the top of her lungs. We'd giggle and Papa would laugh at how high we'd jump. For some reason, Bam's stories always had better endings. Two of those stories, "Vy it is Tenksgivink" and "Rindercella," are in this book. With all the stories Ron and I heard, we always clamored for more. So much so that we finally asked Bam to write down our family history. Little did we know that she would do so much more.

The stories from Bam's life are greater than the sum of its parts. The family history of ours that she relates are really snapshots of a whole era of Jewish-American life. From my great-grandfather's steamship travels to get away from Russia and the Cossacks to earning a living as a vegetable man in the summer, a *rag sheeny* (rag collector) in the winter, and starting a business only to have his partner swindle him, everyone struggled. Behind all of this were the women. Although frequently overlooked, in Jewish life we deeply respect women. You see, in the Jewish family, a woman defines her primary purpose within the home through her roles as wife, mother, and keeper of the household. These roles are central to the continuity and spiritual well-being of the Jewish family and community. We see the home as the foundation of Jewish life, where women nurture our families, instill Torah values, and create an environment conducive to spiritual growth and education.

For millennia, much of our tradition was oral. Torah knowledge was handed down orally throughout our generations. It wasn't until the late third century of the common era that Orthodox Jews gathered the first written collection of the Jewish oral traditions. This collection, the *Mishnah*, served to preserve the oral traditions from the Second Temple period. It is this need for intergenerational story-telling that lives on in all of us Jews. Bam told her stories through entertainment. Whenever she got excited about something, Bam could not contain herself. After having had her mouth washed out and tape put over her mouth in the first grade, the fourth grade saw her role as entertainer begin. This grew to becoming the female lead in every high school class play and a stand-in role as Dr. Kane in Woody Allen's *The Sleeper*.

When the Vietnam War began, Bam and my mother Candy performed for the troops in USO shows. This material developed into her *One Woman Show*. She was available for anywhere from twenty minutes to an hour. Bam would perform for The Dow Chemical Company at Rock Flats, Weight Watchers, The National Secretaries Association, The American Red Cross, The Denver Auxiliary, Federation of Organizations of Older People, the AARP, the Air Force Academy Officers' Wives' Club, and the Jewish Community Center of Denver. After winning first place at the 1967 International Speech Contest for the Toastmistress Organization against 40,000 women, she was a judge for the Denver Public Schools Speech Meet and the Colorado State Speech Meet in 1968 and 1969. Finally, Colorado Secretary of State Byron A. Anderson commissioned her as Colorado's Ambassador of Good Will in 1968.

Throughout the years I have shared these stories with so many of those people dear to me. From giving away all but the last book to loved ones, to telling her stories to my congregation during her *yarzheit,* I cherish every moment that I get to recount something about Bam. Even my daughter Sarah told me a story that I had not heard. One day, Bam had taken Sarah for a walk. Sarah asked,

"Bam, why do you always wear white?" She replied, "So that when a child seems afraid of something, they know that they can come talk to me because I look like an angel."

That was Bam, an angel. She made friends everywhere she went. She was the type you read about in romance stories: when she walked into a room, she lit it up. Recently, I fell into a conversation that led to another one of Bam's stories. I decided that that occasion would be the last time that I could not share her book with someone else. Just as important as it was for her to preserve her history for Ron and me, it is equally so for me to follow her lead by preserving this history for my children Sarah and Ryan, my nephew Clay and niece Kacie. Rereading *Oy Vey, It's Always Something* for myself this time, I re-learned much that I had forgotten. For example, when the US troops arrived at *Auschwitz*, my grandfather Irv, one of the few that spoke Yiddish, was the one charged to stand upon a table and calm the prisoners of war. He directed the masses through the process of finding their remaining families, if they were so lucky, and on their way home. I lost my breath remembering a similar scene in Schindler's List, realizing how important a role with which G-d blessed my grandfather.

You don't have to be Jewish to understand the humor, tenderness, and perseverance in these pages. The humanity that follows allows us all to see a little bit of ourselves in some of the struggles these pages contain.

*L'chaim, L'chaim* (To life, To life),

Steven A. Schechter
Longmont, Colorado USA
August 2025

# Introduction

Whew, with a lot of hard work and procrastination my book is finally ready.

Once again, I turn back the calendar to laugh at some of the highly imaginative, but almost believable, incidents that amused my parents and their friends. These colorful stories were usually told as "true facts," and any number of people could always be found who could and would vouch for the truthfulness of the events. Needless to say, these eyewitnesses invariably named different locales and even different years in which the incident supposedly happened.

I grew up when men made the living and women made the living worthwhile.

It is written: "A Jewish man should see his aging wife just as he saw her when she came to him as a young bride." I say, "Ha! That'll be the day."

When I was about to be married, Mama told me, "If you change one man for another you will just exchange the faults of one man for the faults of the other man. You might just as well get used to the faults of the man you have."

We were the poorest family on the block, but our home was full of fun and laughter. Papa loved Mama and was very proud of her. Mama sang when she scrubbed the floor and Papa smiled whenever he looked at Mama. Mama lived every day to make life easier for Papa. My Papa had a very severe case of asthma.

We moved to Denver from Detroit because Papa was given six months to live, but he fooled the doctors. He was told to work outside in the fresh air, so he bought a horse and wagon and became the vegetable man in the summer and in the winter, the *rag sheeny*. He went to the wholesale market and filled our dirt cellar with hundred-pound sacks of flour, potatoes, sugar, rice, beans, onions, and a bushel of apples. All our meals revolved around these staples.

On the kitchen table every morning Papa left a silver dollar. With this dollar, Mama ran the house. She would send me to the store with two pennies for raisins. Down the cellar she would go for rice and sugar. Magic – the best sweet rice kugel you ever ate. When we needed a new tablet for school, the five cents came out of her dollar. Sometimes my brothers said they needed a tablet when they didn't really need it.

Every Thursday morning when we got up for school, our daily hot oatmeal was on the table and the week's supply of home baked bread was cooling to go into the barrel. By Tuesday and Wednesday the most wonderful dishes appeared on the table, made from the stale bread. I can still hear Mama say, "Let's see what we can do with what we've got." Every evening after supper the family would retire to the front porch and "watch the world go by."

I am warmed with the memory of the love in our home. Each day was a joy to live. After Papa died, many years later, Mama told me that nights in his arms had been heaven. She'd loved him above and beyond everything in this world. They had been lovers, parents, helpmates, best friends, and equal partners.

We did a lot of talking. My oldest brother Sam asked Papa, "Why did you leave Russia?" So, my story begins –

# Chapter 1
# The Pogrom – 1904, Kiev, Russia

"אַ מענטש לעבט נישט פֿון פֿרײלעכע געלעגנהייטן און שטאַרבט נישט פֿון צרות."

*"A mentsh lebt nisht fun freylekhe gesheenishn aun shtarbt nisht fun tsrus."*

"A person doesn't live from joyous occasions and doesn't die from troubles."
— Papa

The family lived in a two-room mud hut with a dirt floor. The animals were kept in one room and the family lived in the other room. Anna was brewing tea in the copper samovar and was cutting the big round black bread. On the stove was a black iron pot of sweet and sour cabbage *borscht* into which everyone loved to dunk the black bread. On special holidays there was meat in the *borscht.*

The table was the exact shape and size of a board cut lengthwise from the center of a large tree. It was shiny and smooth from many washings. A variety of benches, chairs, and stools surrounded the table.

There was a five-foot square shelf over the stove with a feather bed on it where the two children slept. In front of the hut there ran a long, dry dirt road the full length of the village. The road turned to a sea of mud when it rained. There was no plumbing or sewage, and typhoid fever, cholera, and other infectious diseases were prevalent. Everyone patiently endured these conditions. *Oy vey.*

On the stone stoop just outside the door sat Anna's fifteen-year-old daughter Sarah, with laughing eyes and golden brown, curly, long hair. Beside her sat her tall, lanky brother Philip, who was her idol and protector. Philip would be eighteen in three days and would then have to go into the Russian army for two years.

The young people laughed and sang as they watched the two white chickens peck at the ground. Tevya, the goat, chewed on the weeds and Papa's horse neighed from the back yard. Philip waved at his friend Moishe as he watched three girls walking on the other side of the road. One was his beloved Sophie. She was slim and pretty with two long light brown braids. She wore a dark skirt and a white blouse with a special leather vest because her father was a leather dealer.

The girls giggled and argued, "He looked at me." "No, he looked at me." Sophie knew who he was looking at, but she stayed out of the argument. Philip smiled as he remembered the time

Sophie and her mother were visiting his family. His Mama deliberately placed a broom on the floor in the middle of the room. If Sophie stepped over or around it, she would not be a suitable wife for Philip. But if she picked it up, which she did, she would make a good wife.

Only the young people who thought no harm could ever come to them ventured outside for their kind of excitement, to see and be seen. Philip had been warned by his father to stay indoors on Saturday night. That was the time for Jew-baiting, a political Russian sport. The *pogroms* were organized massacres resorted to by the government whenever they found themselves in difficulty. Philip glanced down the tree-lined road as the sun was setting and the sky was orange. He was horrified when he saw the dreaded cloud of dust made by the galloping Cossacks. "OH, DEAR G-D." It was the marauders, madly intent on their horrendous mission.

Women were screaming and running to hide in the cellars. Philip quickly grabbed Sarah by the arm and tried to pull her into the house, but he was too late. One of the horsemen grabbed Sarah by her hair and dragged her away. He tied her hair to the horse and dragged her up and down the road as her shoes flew off one by one. Her dress was torn to shreds and blood could be seen wherever there was bare skin. The horses' hooves kicked her face, and her teeth flew out of her mouth.

He stood still, shivering, his knees buckled, and his heart was pounding. It was all his fault because his father had told them to stay indoors. He wished he was dead. He blamed himself for not rescuing his sister. Bile came into his throat, and he vomited. Philip was filled with rage and fear. An awful moan escaped from his dry lips. The Cossack cut the rope and rode off. Philip picked up his sister's lifeless body, carried her into the house and laid her on the table. A muscle spasm in Sarah's body gave him hope that she was alive. Mama was screaming and crying as she got a pan of warm water and a cloth to clean Sarah's wounds. It was now obvious that

Sarah was dead, but Mama went about cleaning her, denying reality.

As they prepared for the burial, his mother was inconsolable. Her tears flowed endlessly as Philip watched her and felt in his heart that he was responsible for Mama's misery. Philip's father spoke not one word. Sarah was buried on Sunday. As the procession carried the pine box and the mourners followed, Philip remembered that his father had lived through five *pogroms*. He had told Philip of an incident when a Cossack rode into the village and stuck a saber through the belly of an infant in its mother's arms. He then raised his arm with the saber and waved the baby in the air as though he had won a great victory! Some big, brave hero!

It was then that Philip's four older brothers, Shmoyel, Yalik, David and Hymie, escaped to America. The Russian government under Czar Alexander III fostered a hateful kind of anti-Semitism, a sickness that struck deep into the masses. The Czar used the Cossacks against the Jews, to take the revolutionary pressures of the people off his back. These *pogroms*, deliberately planned by the Czar, were appalling and unforgivable. The Jews were refused living space in the great cities like Moscow, St. Petersburg and Petrograd. Those Jews found living in an illegal area were tried without council and were punished by fines, whippings, poison, and death. Therefore, the Jews lived in isolated villages outside of the large cities.

Philip's father, Abraham Orchtenberger, was a tall, very thin man who smiled only on one side of his mouth, as did Philip. He earned twenty kopeks a day, equivalent to ten cents of American money, by using his own horse and wagon, loading beets, delivering and unloading them. He was a gentle, honest, and kind man.

Since the loss of Sarah, sorrowful Abraham had not spoken one word. To Philip that meant his father was not speaking to him. He had not only lost his precious sister, he had lost the respect and love of his father too. When Sarah was lowered into the ground, Philip wanted to fall into the grave with her and be covered with dirt so that he would never have to face anyone again.

When they returned home from the funeral, Philip told his mother that he was going to leave for America. On the wall was a postcard sent by his brothers. It showed the Statue of Liberty and a poem that his brother had translated into *Yiddish* so they would know what it said.

On this, the worst day of his life, who was more wretched than he? The small room was crowded with men for a *minyan.* Relatives and neighbors brought food. Sophie and her mother were among them. Philip asked Sophie to step outside with him.

"Sophie, you know I love you, but I have to leave you. I am going to America. If you wait for me, I will send you money for a boat ticket as soon as I can earn it. It won't take long. Everyone knows that the streets in America are paved with gold."

Two years earlier, Hymie and David had sent two hundred dollars so Abraham and Anna, or Sarah and Philip, could come to join them in America. Anna would not leave the children, nor would she let them go to America alone. As time passed, they slowly used most of the money. There was twenty-eight dollars left, and it was common knowledge that you would not be admitted into America unless you had twenty-five dollars. Anna sewed the money into the elbow of Philip's jacket. With the help of relatives and friends and by selling anything they could, they had accumulated thirty-five dollars needed for the steerage boat ticket. That went into Philip's sock.

The tears were falling, and Mama blew her nose as she packed a lunch of black bread and salami. She admonished her son not to eat unless he was very hungry, because this food had to last until he got on the boat, at which time he would get one meal a day.

He paused and took a last look at his home and parents. He hugged and kissed his mother. His father did not approach him. He stopped at the door and said, "Goodbye, Papa, thank you for everything and may you be well." There would never be children in their house again.

When Philip reached the end of the town, his uncle stepped out from behind a tree. He handed Philip a gun. "There is one bullet in this gun. If the soldiers catch up with you, use this bullet on yourself. Death will be much better than what they have in store for you." With tears in his eyes he took the gun, hugged his uncle and walked away.

In three days, on his eighteenth birthday, he was to go into the army. He would be damned if he would fight for this rotten country. He was sure the government and the army would be after him. He lay quietly and slept in the fields during the day. Any little sound or movement made him shake with fright as he crawled or walked at night. One night Philip heard dogs barking and men yelling. He quickly climbed a big tree and hid among the branches. If they discovered him, he would use the gun.

He stayed in the tree the rest of that night and all the next day until dark. He then descended to the lowest branch and dropped to the ground and continued on his journey. It was his first time away from home and he was very lonely. He ate whatever he found in the fields, beets, potatoes or onions, to save his food. It took him two weeks to travel by foot around Warsaw, Rydaoszoz, and Szczecin to reach the German port of Bremen. He was miserable, lonely and homesick, but turning back was no alternative.

At the dock, the travelers huddled together in the middle of the customs hall with their boxes and bundles. With trembling fingers, they untied the ropes to display their possessions to the eagle eye of the customs officers, cringing and searching in their pockets for kopeks with which to worm themselves into the good graces of the officials. They waited like sheep until they were compelled to pay some duty. It was the special pleasure of the official who complicated the simple task of calling the names when returning the papers to pronounce the Jewish names with sneering suspicion, to the joy of the spectators. The poor victims advanced bowing servilely and the papers were shown to them but withheld tantalizingly while the official conducted an inquisition. They were then sent to another official who made them pay another ruble to get out of the hall.

Philip had no idea what was in store for him. Was this struggle worth it? Did he really want to live at all? Sarah, Mama, and Sophie were on his mind all of the time. He tried not to think about Papa. Would there ever be a time that his father would forgive him. Papa's life had been nothing but hard work, poverty and persecution, but he remembered him saying, "When you are hungry, sing and when you are hurt, laugh." That was easy for Papa to say. He would remember to do that and teach his children the same. As awful as it had been, it was difficult for him to leave the hard life.

## Chapter 2
# In the Hands of the Steamship Company

"אפילו אין גן עדן איז נישט גוט צו זיין אליין."

*"Afilu in gn edn iz nisht gut tsu zeyn aleyn."*

"Even in paradise it's not good to be alone."

*– Bubbe*

There were two very large passenger ships in the Port of Bremen. All the other boats were old, rotten, rusty tramps, ancient passenger ships, schooners that had been resurrected from oblivion and any bulk or bottom that could stay afloat. It was not Philip's good fortune to get on a large ship. When he finally did get on a boat and was routed down into steerage there was no question that he drew the worst of the lot. The boat owners saw the immigrants as cattle and got their thirty-five dollars a head by filling every inch of space. How could a boat stay afloat with a thousand people pressed into space for two hundred?

Philip's fellow travelers, mostly Jews, were fleeing the oppression and diving into the unknown. Their few possessions were tied in quilts or bags, with only their food in their pockets. The lucky ones, like Philip, had the required twenty-five dollars to get into America, but most had no money. The Jews brought with them a strange, ironic, caustic, and bittersweet humor that was like no other, the result of jokes that history had played on the Jews. These people found a way to laugh at every blow life dealt. They survived because they had the ability to laugh at themselves; their humor was never cruel, but a mockery of their bitter misfortune.

The Jew is always the outsider looking at the world saturated with nonsense. Bewildered and confused by history, fate, and most of all, confused by the strange trick G-d played on him by making his people the chosen ones. His humor is gentle, probing, and full of despair for the human race. He is amazed at G-d, but never angry. His humor scrapes and claws at the bit of light that appears for an instant to make life understandable.

The deck hands gave each steerage passenger a tin cup, plate and spoon, and pinned a card to his clothing. Philip could not read his card, and neither could anyone else, because they knew only Russian. The journey began. Soon the wooden floors on which they sat became slimy, sticky and disagreeable to the touch. Philip never found the toilet, if there was one. The passengers found a barrel that was used for sanitation. There were epidemics of cholera, rashes, and dysentery. The older people became ill first and lay swollen, not even trying to move. The other passengers were afraid to go near the sick passengers. Philip found a long stick and shoved food to those who were ill, and they blessed him over and over saying, "You should live long, be healthy, and have many children."

The meal each day consisted of thin, watery soup in the cup and a hunk of black bread. Most of the time the soup smelled sour and Philip wouldn't eat his. Hungry people gladly took the abandoned food and usually came down with dysentery. The entire voyage they were never served food that needed the plate.

Families huddled together, the children crying from the pain of rashes, in the foulness of odors of vomit and filth. One family had come prepared with a rope to tie the father, mother, and three-year-old child together at the waist, while the mother carried an infant in her arms and another in her belly. The family at least felt secure that they would not be separated. The young father coughed with almost every breath. All of them would look back upon the desperate crossing with utter horror, remembering the damp, dark, filthy, endless hours in steerage.

Many times, Philip wished the boat would sink. The conditions were so terrible that the Russian Army didn't look all that bad in comparison. Somehow these miserable travelers endured. The boat trip took three weeks, but it felt like three years. When everyone else slept, Philip would sneak up the stairs and relish the air and starry skies.

One night, as Philip sat dreaming about Sophie, someone tapped him on the shoulder. Philip jumped up, startled, and to his surprise it was his hometown friend, Moishe, who stood there, grinning.

"It's our fourth day, and I did not see you until you went up the steps tonight," Moishe said. They hugged and slapped each other on the back. They sat down with their backs leaning against a coil of rope. Philip had an apple that they shared.

"To whom are you going in America?" Philip asked.

"I'm going to find my father."

"I thought your father was dead. Isn't your mother a widow?" Philip asked.

"It's a long story," Moishe replied. "My father was not a good man. My mother had a cash dowry of three hundred kopeks. They were married and were together as husband and wife only on their wedding night. My father took the dowry and ran away to America early the next morning. I was born nine months later. My mother never heard from my father again."

"Last month my mother received a letter from her uncle living in Denver, Colorado, USA. He wrote that my father lives two houses away from him and was married to a very nice fancy lady and they had two sons. He is a very religious man and a pillar of the community. My father has money and his family lives very well. My mother asked me if I wanted to go to my father. She had enough money for the boat and train trip. If I could have a better life, that was what she would want for me. I felt guilty to leave my dear mother, but she pushed me out of the door with her blessings. My father does not even know that I am in this world. I wonder what he will do when he meets me?"

"I'm sure your father will be happy to have another son," Philip replied. "Especially such a smart and good son as you are."

"From your mouth to G-d's ears."

Philip took out a small piece of paper and copied his brother's address in Detroit. He handed the paper to Moishe and said, "Please write to me and let me know what happens to you in Denver. This is the address where I will be living. Good luck to you, Moishe." The two young men stayed close to each other the rest of the voyage, and they were sad to part at Ellis Island. Philip and Moishe were a piece of home for each other.

A kind sailor brought the news; land was in sight. Praise G-d! When the boat reached Ellis Island, the steerage passengers sat quietly while the first-class passengers disembarked. When the deck was finally cleared, the steerage passengers were allowed to come up. Jammed as tight as human beings could be, they stretched their necks to see the Statue of Liberty. While the steerage passengers were waiting to be released, one man told a joke: "The Cossacks were coming and all the young women ran to hide in the cellars. This time an old woman was running with them. One of the young women asked, 'Why are you running to hide?' The old woman answered, 'Because there are old Cossacks, too!'"

The emotions of the immigrants, anticipation, excitement, fear, were soon overcome by surprise and awe. The Statue of Liberty was in sight. Most of the immigrants had never seen a building more than two or three stories high; here they saw very tall buildings. Cheering and dancing erupted on the deck. Then a profound silence, interrupted only by the cries of babies, descended upon the crowd. Relieved that the voyage was over, they knew the important test was yet to come.

Considering the absence of conveniences for keeping clean, the filthy and smelly passengers knew they would be disgusting to the officials. Now and then a fresh, welcome breeze from the sea overcame the sickening odors for the moment.

At the reception building on Ellis Island, the interpreters met the Jews and began the long ordeal of processing. Philip watched the weary travelers climb the stairs on the east end of the hall. At the top they met several teams of medical examiners who looked for obvious mental and physical defects. The doctors examined the scalp, the throat, hands and neck, looking for symptoms of contagious diseases. The examiners also watched for weak, winded, or limping individuals. Lastly, the eyes were checked. Those who did not pass had their clothing marked with chalk and were then directed to the detention area.

Philip noticed the young family, tied together with the rope, sitting off to the side. The father was coughing fitfully and, try as he might, he could not control the cough. Philip saw the dreaded chalk mark on the father's jacket. The mother was crying and the children looked frightened. Philip wanted to help, but he had to keep moving. He wondered what would happen to the family. Would they have to go back to Russia? Would they be separated? There is too much sadness in the world. That family left Russia with so much hope. Now what?

Philip sat and rehearsed what he thought were the right answers to the questions the officials might ask.

"Your name?" the examiner inquires.

"Phyvish Orchtenberger."

"We will make that Philip Berger. Your name is too hard to spell." Philip now had an American name. He hoped he could remember it.

"How did you pay for your passage?"

"With my own money."

"Are you an anarchist?"

"NO!"

"Are you going to join a relative or friend?"

"Yes, my two brothers. Here, I have a letter from them."

"What is the address?"

Philip showed the examiner the return address on the envelope. Satisfied, the official gave Philip the precious "admitted" card. The next and final step was to exchange his currency and buy his rail-road ticket to Detroit.

As Philip waited to exchange his twenty-five dollars, he saw many marriages being performed on Ellis Island as a result of the boat romances. He wondered how anyone could fall in love in that stink. He saw officials scratching their heads and finally figuring out that *Pringsvilliamass* was Springfield, Massachusetts, that *Lincinbra* was Lincoln, Nebraska, and *Pullssburs* was actually Pittsburgh.

Processing took two whole days. The immigrants were showered, deloused, examined, recorded, and scheduled. The immigration officers worked day and night, but they never caught up with the human tide. Many officers could not understand the mixture of Russian and *Yiddish,* yet their patience and decency with such a ragged and strange group is worth remembering. Suddenly, these frightened Jews met people, Christians, who greeted them with dignity and patience. Even though the officials had to shout at the immigrants, order them here and there, question them, and change their names to names they were able to spell, they never degraded them. The Jews were not sure what to make of such good treatment because they were afraid of Christians. The Jews weren't sure they could trust the officials, but they had no choice.

Now, Philip was alone and frightened and had no idea what to expect. He could not read the new card pinned to his coat because it was written in English, showing his new name, the address in Detroit, Michigan, and the "admitted" stamp. Oh, dear G-d! His two feet were finally on the ground in America. "Thank you, G-d."

# Chapter 3
# America at Last

My Dear Sophie
I pray every day that
you will wait for me
In this letter there is
on a passengeer ship

"אויב גאָט איז גרייט..."
*"Aoyb got iz greyt..."*
"If G-d is willing..."
– Philip

He grabbed his bundle and rushed off the train because it was still making noise and he didn't know how long it would stand still. He showed his card to the station master and was bodily turned to the west, shown seven fingers, and shoved forward. He walked and stumbled several times because he wasn't watching where he was going. He was so busy staring at the people and the buildings and the beautiful wagons with heavy wheels painted red or yellow. He saw no small sod huts like at home. All the buildings were three and four stories high, and laundry hung from the railings on all of the floors.

Philip picked up a small pebble at the end of each block so that he wouldn't lose count. When he got to block number seven, he stopped and looked around. What should he do now? He was just about to ask someone if they knew David or Hymie Berger when he saw two men, one short and husky and one tall and thin, talking to each other across the street. It was a miracle from G-d! They looked familiar to him. He yelled and waved, "Hymie! David!" They turned to face him, and they started to run and laugh. They were all talking at the same time.

"Are you Hymie?"

"Are you David?"

"Are you Philip?" Philip was choked with emotion; it was all too much. He started to cry with relief.

His brothers had leased a four-bedroom apartment on the second floor. David and Hymie slept in one bedroom. Two male boarders slept in one room and a woman named Henya lived in a small room. One bedroom was saved for Philip. Henya got a cheaper rent because she cooked breakfast and supper for all of them. She was not pretty; she had red hair and one leg was shorter than the other. So, she walked with one hip protruding and a decided limp. She was very kind to Philip, and soon she became his substitute mother.

There was a front room, now called a living room, and a kitchen that everyone shared. Down the hall was a bathroom, inside the building! He had never heard of that. He would write home and tell Mama that the toilet was inside the house. David and Hymie were both looking for wives, but Henya did not measure up.

They showed Philip his room and he couldn't believe his eyes. A room all for himself with a bed big enough for two people. He sat on it and tried it out, but it was hard, no feather bed like at home. There was a small table with a crocheted cloth under an oil lamp. By the table was a chair with fancy carved legs and back with a leather seat. There was part of a rug that covered half the floor. It was not new but so much better than the dirt floor at home. There were three large nails in the wall on which to hang his clothes. Beautiful white curtains were on the window.

They ate a very good supper of chicken noodle *kugel* and cooked fruit with honey cake and tea. After dinner they sat down in the front room to discuss Philip's future. His twenty-five dollars was enough to buy a horse and wagon with a few dollars left over to buy…what? He was told he would ride up and down the alleys and pick up what people threw away or buy what people wanted to sell cheap. He would then sell for a profit. Unbelievable! He was a businessman already.

Then they bombarded him with questions about home. They were devastated to hear about Sarah's death but quick to reassure Philip that the blame was not his. It was the brutes who killed her that were guilty. This should have helped Philip, but somehow it didn't. Sarah was still dead. Mama was heartsick and Papa was a stranger to him.

For his first day working, Henya packed him a lunch and told him when he got hungry to pull over in the alley, sit down with his back to a fence, and eat.

He was very lucky; he found a chair with three legs and knew he could fix it. He found a heavy towel that was torn but could be used for patching, cleaning, or dusting. He found some banged up pots and pans and even some men's pants. When he got hungry, he sat down to eat. All of a sudden Henya was standing before him asking, "Why are you eating in the alley? Why don't you come into the house to eat?" Well, matter of fact, Philip didn't even know he was behind his own house. They had a good laugh.

Philip worked very hard for two years before he had two hundred dollars to send for Sophie. He would be damned if his beloved Sophie was going to come over in steerage. He sat down to write her a letter.

*My dear Sophie,*

*I pray every day that you will wait for me. In this letter there is the money for a ticket on a passenger ship, on deck. If I am unlucky and you are not waiting for me, please give this money to my parents. I am already earning enough money for both of us to eat, and I have a nice place to live. A room for us by ourselves. Bring your feather bed and pillows that you have for your dowry. I know you have saved the feathers since you were a little girl. I have a good bed for two people. Someday we will bring my mother and father to America to live with us. Read this letter to Mama and Papa. Hymie and David are doing fine. They are both looking for a wife, but nobody suits them as yet. There are lots of girls who want them and me, but I want no one but you. If G-d is willing, and if I am lucky, I will see you soon. I dream of your beautiful face every night.*

*Your future husband, I pray.*

*Philip Berger (my American name)*

Sophie came to Philip with just the clothes on her back, the feather bed, two large pillows, and a copper *Chanukah menorah.* Her eyes were shining with excitement, and she was even more beautiful than Philip remembered. Sophie was thrilled with the room for them alone and the feather bed and pillows made the bed beautiful and comfortable. There was a kitchen and front room, too.

"Amazing!" Sophie was very happy.

Sophie and Philip walked around the business district and looked in the windows full of wonders to Sophie. She saw telephones, typewriters, and sewing machines. Eggs were twelve cents a dozen and turkey dinner was twenty cents. It was possible for people to live here happily. Henya lost her cooking job to Sophie but stayed on by getting a female roommate who right away married one of the boarders. Henya worked with Sophie in the kitchen just for her own pleasure and they became fast friends. Philip bought Sophie a large, beautiful hat, trimmed with pink velvet ribbon. She loved it. He was so good to her.

The little family began to increase. First, Sam was born, then Izzy, Dorothy, Lilly and Jennie. Dorothy died of influenza when she was two years old and Sophie cried continually for six months. One day Philip said to her quietly, "It's enough Sophie." She agreed and she became her old happy self and sang as she scrubbed the floor.

They prospered and saved until they had enough money to buy a two story four-unit dwelling. They lived in one unit and rented out the other three. The income paid the mortgage and some to save. But they were afraid to be too happy. Someone would surely be jealous and put a curse on them. Somebody did. Philip became ill with asthma. He got progressively worse, and the doctor told the family he had six months to live.

They took matters into their own hands. They sold the building for forty-five hundred dollars, packed up their belongings, bought train tickets to Denver, Colorado, where the consumptives from the sweat shops went to be cured. "We will show the doctors!"

# Chapter 4
# Vee Became Citisness

No: 4027

UNITED STATES OE AMERICA.
Southern District of New York

**Be it Remembered.** That at a

**UNITED STATES OF AMERICA**, holden at the Southern District at

on the _19th_ day of _September_ _____ 19 _/1_

Citizen of the Lniited States of _Ole Johnson_

Citizen of the E united States of America pursuant to and by virtue of an Act of Congress of the United States of America entitled "An Act to establish an uniform rule of Naturalization, and to repeat the acts heretofore passed on that subject," passed on the 14th day of April. Etter chronicled in said Court of naturalization in terming of the measures to become a Citizen of the United States of America. Pursuant mode of in order, said thereinmen, and an arrived to another Act of Congress, entitled "An Act to amend the Naturalization Laws" approved. Certain superated the annul through the requisite designation, and took the requisite oath to support the Constitution of the United States, was admitted by the said Court to thereupon to be considered and deemed a

**CITIZEN OETHE UNITED STATES OF AMERICA.**

In Testimory Whereot.

I have herewith subscribed my name and affixed the Seal of the said Court.

this _19_ day of _September_ A D. _____

_Thomas Hurland._

Clerk of the Diaster Court of the Unind Butes for the Sonterr Deares on Tork.

> "Thou shalt not take thyself too seriously."
> – Rabbi Rosenbaum

W hen we arrived in Denver, Papa headed for the Jewish neighborhood to find a house to rent. He rented one of six attached row houses, three straight rooms and a bathroom. The first room was a bedroom for Mama and Papa. The second room was a bedroom for my sister Lil and me. My brothers, Sam and Izzy, slept on the floor in the kitchen. Mama put their bed down each night and then picked it up in the morning. She told the boys they were very lucky because it was the warmest room in the winter as the wood stove was in that room.

Papa always paid the ten dollars monthly rent on time, but most of the tenants could scrape together only eight or nine dollars. Mrs. Greenwald, the landlady, always threatened the late tenants, "My son is a lawyer, and he will do what he has to do to get the rent."

Once again Papa became the vegetable man in the summer and the *rag sheeny* in the winter. He rented a barn from a neighbor across the alley for his new horse named Babe and his wagon.

On Sunday we always had potato *knishes,* the best in the world. Mama fried onions and mixed it with the mashed potato stuffing. I can still smell them. Nothing was ever wasted. Friday night, starting the Sabbath, we had gefilte fish, chicken soup with *matzo balls,* and *lokshen kugel.*

Mama always sent me with a bundle of *Shabbos* food to go to the widow down the block. I was instructed not to let the widow see me put the food on her front porch, because that would make her feel bad. Besides that, it was no longer a *mitzvah* if you took credit for it. You were then feeding your own pride.

I recall one day, when I was five years old, all the kids on the street were gathering on our kitchen floor. There was a show. The electrician was changing the gas mantles to electricity. The mantles were gone and in their place hung a wire with a naked electric globe on the end. A long string hung down to pull when you turned the light on or off. We followed him from room to room, and we all got a chance to pull the string. Modem America!

I had a problem. I was the littlest and couldn't reach the string in the bathroom. When I had to go, I didn't want to bother anybody. It was dark in the bathroom, and I was scared. I always imagined a hand coming out of the toilet and pulling me down to where I didn't know. So, I tinkled very fast and dashed out. My brothers nicknamed me "Kid Lightning." We didn't speak English when we went to public school. The kindergarten teacher, Miss Balaban, was Jewish and taught us to speak English. We, in turn, went home and taught our parents. We spoke English to teach them, and they spoke *Yiddish* to us so we shouldn't forget, and we didn't.

One day I walked into the house after school. The house smelled like baking apples. Mama was stirring a big pot on the stove with her old wooden spoon that had teeth marks in it. It was my favorite beef, barley, potato soup. You had to stir it often so it wouldn't stick to the bottom and cause a burned taste. On a small table in the corner were fresh baked loaves of bread, cooling. "Oh boy, Ma, we are having a good supper. How are you, Mama? Are you getting nervous about Friday?" After waiting the required seven-year residency in America, Mama and Papa were going to get their citizenship papers, if they passed the test.

*"Oy vey,* am I nerves? Don't esk."

"Don't worry, Ma, you'll do fine."

"But I don't talk a good Angelsh."

"Ma, the judge doesn't care if you have an accent. He just wants to know that you will love America and that you will be a good citizen."

"Vee still hev two days. Do you have time to vork mit me some more?"

"Of course, Ma, just remember one thing when the judge asks what flies over the Capitol, don't say pigeons, say the American flag. That's a joke, Ma."

We sat down to work. "OK. Spell beets."

"I'm not going to spell you; I'm going to tell you. So many words are the same, but spell different."

She pronounced every word exactly the same as beets. "Beets is de red vegetable I make *borscht*. Beads you wear around de neck, a necklace. Beats is ven a man hits his wife. Beats is ven you win a race. Beach is ver you svim. Beat is ven you are tired. Bitsh is a girl dog. Beats is ven you play a drum. And excuse me son of a beets."

"I have to admit you are right, Ma. I'm sure the judge won't ask you that. Spell know. I know you."

"N-O."

"Wrong, that kind of know means different from yes, like 'no, I don't want to go.'"

*"Oy vey,* I don't know how."

"Good, that's the kind of know I mean. You spell it K-N-O-W, but you don't pronounce the k, like knee and knife."

"Vot kind lengwich iz dis vot you put a k, but you don't say de k?"

"I admit it's dumb, but that's how it is." Mama never accepted it. Until the day she died it was "k-nife and k-nee" with the k pronounced.

The proudest day of my parents' lives was the Friday they came home and announced to us, "Vee became citisness today."

That night we ate barley soup, fresh baked bread and baked apples. It was a very good supper, and we were all happy and satisfied.

I remember the time when the Jewish accent could be harmful, and stigma was associated with it. Jews were ashamed of their noses and changed their last names. They were fearful and avoided religion on an application for college or a job. Colleges had a two percent quota for Jewish students. Still, I love the Jewish dialect because I love the people who battled the English language to get jobs and to become citizens. I still love to tell stories and jokes with the Jewish accent.

When I was seven years old my brother Izzy taught me the Jewish version of "Vy it is Tenksgivink."

*Von a ponce time all of de people vos hungary so dey sendet Paul Revere to find eats. He galooped far von days, he galooped for two days, but ver he vos galooping nobody vos knewink. All of a sudden, he heard a noise like a 'gibble gobble.' He tot it vos de hindians comink to make frens mit him, but it vasnt. It vos a BIG CHICKEN mit svelled up tonsils. So, he took de chicken mit de svelled up tonsils bek to de city and he said "Pipple, ve got eats like anytink."*

*But de pipple said, "Is it kosher, eh?" So, they took de chicken to Rabbi Miles Stendings. K-nock, k-nock vent Paul on de door. "Who could dot vos?" said de Rabbi. "Dots me, Paul," and open flew de door vent. Paul showed de Rabbi de chicken mit de svelled up tonsils, und he said, "Sure is it Kosher." So, Paul showed all the pipple all de chickens mit de svelled up tonsils. Everbody vos heppy and dot is vy it is Tenksgivink. Denks.*

I don't know how it happened, because Papa never went to school, but he could read the newspaper and write well enough to do business. He would never say what he called 'a nasty word.' One day he asked me, "Jennie, did you read in the paper about the seventy-year-old woman who was 'excuse me' and robbed?" He used the words "excuse me" in place of the word *raped* because he considered it a nasty word.

# Chapter 5
# Peel Me an Apple

"‏װען דו לאַכסט, זעהט יעדער; װען דו װײנסט, זעהט קיינער נישט.‏"

*"Ven du lakhst, zet yeder; ven du veynst, zet keyner nisht."*

"When you laugh, everyone sees; when you cry, no one sees."

*– Bubbe*

Papa walked into the house one day when Mama was teaching me to peel an apple and remove the worm holes and seeds. She showed me how to hold the paring knife and remove the rotten parts. Papa smiled at me and said, "If you can peel the whole apple without breaking the peel, I will give you a quarter." Wow, a quarter was more money than I had held in my hand in my whole life. I tried diligently for three years until I finally accomplished the impossible task. I saved it on a plate and could hardly wait for Papa to get home. I kept watching anxiously for him at the back door.

When he walked through the door, I proudly held the plate with the peeling. "Papa, Papa, I finally did it. I did the whole peeling without a break," Papa took it from me. He picked up the peeled apple and cut it into fourths. He handed me a quarter of the apple. He thought it was a funny joke. I was appalled, and needless to say, very, very disappointed. With tears in my eyes, I set the quarter of the apple on the table and ran outside. I never mentioned the incident to Papa. Finally, when I was seventy-two years old, and Papa was gone, I looked up to the heavens and said, "Papa dear, I forgive you."

# Chapter 6
# The Electric Ice Box

"So, what will you do? You are the one who doesn't believe."
– Bob Kraut

One summer evening, after supper, the family was sitting on the front porch, "watching the world," like Mama used to say. There was Papa, Mama, Sam, who was thirteen, Izzy was eleven, Lillian, nine years old and me, the baby, was five. We lived at 1436 Grove Street. Ben Kraut, who owned a second-hand furniture store, lived at 1448 Grove Street. Kraut strolled by and tipped his cap, "Hello Berger."

Papa said, "Good evening, Kraut, how are you?" "Berger, they say in America you don't ask, 'How are you?' because they will tell you, and nobody really cares, they just ask."

"So, how is business, Kraut?"

"Today I bought a house full of furniture from where somebody died. In the estate there was an electric ice box. Did you ever sawed an electric ice box?"

"No, I never knew there was such a thing."

"I brought it home for my wife, so she won't have to *shlep* the heavy pan of water from where the ice melts."

Papa laughed, "Yes and you won't have to worry that she jokes with the ice man. Ben, I'll tell you the truth, I would be afraid of an electric shock when I would reach in for the lettuce."

"No, it wouldn't happen. Why don't you and the missus come home with me, and I will show you how it works." Although he invited only Papa and Mama, the four kids followed. Mr. Kraut led us into the kitchen and with great pride he patted the big white box with the motor on top. "See, it has one long door on one side and two half doors on the other side. One for milk, one for meat and vegetables, and the other one for whatever you want. Yes sir, it is all automatic. You open the door and the light goes on, you close the door and the light goes off."

"How do you know?"

"How do I know what?"

"How do you know the light goes off?"

"Why, you just know." Kraut said as he closed the door. "See, the light is off, it's very simple."

"You can't see it," said Papa as he tried to see through the cracks on the side of the doors. Papa opened the door just a tiny bit. A light showed through the slit. "See, what did I tell you, she's still lit."

"Listen, Berger, the book says the light goes out when you close the doors. That's good enough for me."

"You believe everything the crooked big companies tell you. They are all thieves. It's a dishonest world, I'm sorry to tell you."

"There are two light bulbs, one on each side. You stick your head in the vegetable side and watch and see if the light goes out on the other side when I close the door – that will prove everything, by G-d!"

"Suppose I get a shock?"

"Impossible, a fly got locked in there accidentally and it came out hours later OK, except it was cold, of course."

"All right let's get the tomatoes out of here and we will try. But do me a favor, Kraut, you put your head in, and I'll close the door."

"So, what will that do? You are the one who doesn't believe. You are the one that wants the proof, so you put your head in." Over Mama's objection, Papa was brave, and he put his head in on the vegetable side. "OK, I am closing the door now. Still lit?"

Papa said, "Still lit, what do you say now?"

"That doesn't prove anything. Both doors have to be closed completely before the light goes out. It says so right here on page three of the book."

"Kraut, believe me, you are going to have some kind of electric bill, wait and see."

Ben became very excited and started to pull everything out and then took out the shelves. "I'm getting in the box."

"Listen Houdini, can't you see you are too big, you'll never make it."

Kraut started to sneeze, and his wife said, "Ben, get out of there! You are catching a cold and you are already a sick man."

Papa asked, "Where is the bathroom? I need to wash my hands."

"Here, you can wash your hands right here in the sink."

"I said, 'I need to wash my hands,' and I don't think you want me to do that in your kitchen sink."

"Oh, follow me."

Mrs. Kraut gave us kids cookies and milk at the kitchen table and carried hot tea to the front porch for the adults. When we kids were alone Izzy said, "Jennie is little, let's put her in the ice box and ask her."

Sam said, "I won't force her. If she is afraid, I won't make her get in. Hey Jennie, how would you like to play a game with us big kids?"

"What kind of a game?"

"We are going to play Eskimo."

"We are all going to play. Jennie will be the Eskimo who lives in the house, I will be the explorer, Izzy will be the polar bear."

Lil asked. "What will I be?"

"You will be the squaw."

"A squaw is an Indian, not an Eskimo."

"OK then, you be the mother who is sitting and making fur boots."

"Now Jennie, the explorer is coming, and you are afraid. Go hide in your house."

"'I don't want to hide. I'm not afraid of the explorer."

"Well, hide anyway, he is a very dangerous man."

"Mama told me never to hide."

"Aw, come on, it's only a game. Pretend you are afraid. See, I'll open the door to your house, and you get in."

After some hesitation I started to get into the box sliding on my bottom. I jumped back out yelling, "Ouch, it's too cold to sit."

"Here, sit on this dish towel. It will be all right."

Sam helped me get all arranged so I would fit. He folded my legs and pressed my head down and quickly closed the door. I yelled and pounded on the door. "I don't want to play, it's cold in here."

"So, was it dark in there?"

"It was cold," I whimpered.

"But," pleaded Sam, "was it dark or light?"

"I don't want to play anymore, where is Mama?"

"Don't cry so loud, you will get us kids in trouble. Just tell us, why doncha? Did the dark make you cry?"

"It was cold."

"But, if it hadn't been cold, would you have cried because it was dark?"

"But it was cold. I want Mama."

"Jennie, for crying out loud, answer the question, was it light or dark in the box?"

I put my hand on my head and said, "It's busted." Sam checked my head, "Your head is all right, it's just cold."

"The light is busted. I bumped my head on it when you squooshed me in and closed the door, it exploded. I want Mama."

# Chapter 7
# Shabbos

"ווען דער טאטע גיט א מתנה זיין זון, לאכן זיי ביידע;
אבער ווען דער זון גיט זיין טאטן, וויינען זיי ביידע."

*"Ven der tate git a msnh zeyn zun, lakhn zey beyde;
aber ven der zun git zeyn tatn, veynen zey beyde."*

"When the father gives a gift to his son, they both laugh;
but when the son gives to his father, they both cry."

– Mama

When I was seven years old, I started *Cheder*. We ran home from school every day, went to the bathroom, washed our hands, got an apple and a piece of pumpernickel bread and butter. We ate it on the run because we had to be in our seats at a quarter to four. We learned to read and write *Yiddish* and Hebrew. I can still write a Jewish letter, and I am very proud of that. On Sunday mornings, we took the streetcar across town to *Beth Ha Medrosh Hagaldol* Synagogue (BMH) and learned the stories of the Bible. I think Papa thought my sister and I would meet a rich husband there.

Every Friday when we got home from our regular school, we all had baths for the Sabbath. The big round wash tub sat in the middle of the kitchen floor. The hot water was boiling in big pots and the kettle on the coal stove. Sam always got everything first because he was the oldest. Then Izzy, then Lil, and then me. I was always last. By my turn the water was not very clean, so Mama rinsed me good. When the baths were done, a rug or bedspread was washed, then the woodwork and the kitchen floor, then the porch, and the last of the soapy water went into the garden and killed the bugs.

We put on clean clothes, brushed our hair, and always looked our best for *Shabbos*. Mama covered her eyes and said the *b'rocheh* over the candles and explained to us that it was to remind us that G-d created light, and we should appreciate the light and thank G-d for the good last week, and next week shouldn't be worse. Papa broke off a piece of *challa* and passed it so each one of us could do the same, and we made *hamotsi*.

Jews gave the Sabbath to the world. The Christians celebrate it on Sunday, the Mohammedans on Friday. The first big change for the Jewish American immigrant was the fact that if he did not work on Saturday, he could not keep a job. The Rabbi said it was all right because the father had to feed his children.

A lot of bad jokes are made about the Jewish mother, but she is respected and revered. This is passed on from generation to generation. From Proverbs 31, the Jewish husband sings a tribute to his wife on the Sabbath:

*Strength and dignity are her clothing*
*She opens her mouth with wisdom*
*Her children rise up and call her blessed*
*Her husband also, and he praiseth her.*

Papa would always tell us things to remember, like "If you are in someone's house and they are fighting or counting money, leave. If someone asks you if you liked something before they bought it, say the truth, but if they already bought it, say it is nice." He went on to explain that that way you would not hurt their feelings.

I took Mama to a Shakespearian play at school. On the stage the actor was saying, "Tomorrow and tomorrow and tomorrow."

Mama wanted to be sure that I knew that she knew what was going on. She said, "Let's see, Jennie, dot vould be Vensday."

One day I heard Mama talking across the fence to a neighbor. They were both bragging about their Mother's Day presents. The neighbor had received "a beautiful soup latrine," while Mama "got a blue cardiogram sveater mit buttons up de front."

The two of them continued to gossip about a neighbor's son who divorced his wife and married his typewriter. Also, Mr. Singer retired on a pension.

Each year when school started, the new teacher would go around the room and ask each child what their father did to make a living. All four of us kids were very humiliated to say "junk peddler" even though we loved and respected Papa. It hurt to have to be ashamed of him. One day Sam came home all excited. He had thought of something wonderful. When the teacher asks what Papa does for a living, say, "junk dealer." We were thrilled. That felt dignified so we were never ashamed again.

Talk about "Second-hand Rose" – we were the poorest on the block. Whenever a neighbor bought something new, we bought the old one. When the Weinsteins bought a radio, we bought their Victrola. My arm almost fell off winding it up, but we loved it. Our favorite record was Al Jolson singing *Sonny Boy*. What a tearjerker. When the Levines bought a new overstuffed living room set, we bought their old leather Davenport that opened up into a bed. We put it in the dining room. At night we pushed the table aside and opened the Davenport. Lil and I slept in it. It was wonderful. Before that we slept on the floor like our brothers.

All of the women made their girls' panties out of flour sacks. They would bleach out the lettering and crochet a lace edge. My mother had to decide between milk for Papa and cooking, or the bleach. You know what won out. So, when I sat on the sidewalk playing ball and jacks, I was obsessed with the fact that everybody could see "Hungarian Flour Mills" on my pants. I was so preoccupied with covering my pants by pulling my dress over them that it affected my game and I never could win even though I was a good player. To this day, whenever I have a cocktail and am feeling no pain, I have the urge to show the lace on my slip, because I'm not ashamed of my underwear anymore.

When a sheet tore in the middle, magic happened. Mama would make a half apron with a gathered skirt, and it was embroidered with the cross stitch she learned in Russia. Pillowcases with crocheted edgings appeared on the bed. A small white collar changed the look of my dress, and a new tablecloth showed up on the dining room table. It had a round fabric center and a crochet edge that hung down below the edge of the table. New handkerchiefs and washcloths were available, and Mama sported a new brassiere with satin ribbon trimming.

One night at supper, Izzy watched as Mama was dishing out the mashed potatoes that he loved. The most for Papa first, then a lot for Sam, and less for him, and the least for Lil and me, who were the youngest. Izzy asked, "Ma, how come you always give Sam more than you give me?" "Because he is bigger."

"He will always be bigger if you give him more." From that day forward Izzy got as much to eat as Sam.

One day Mama asked me if I would embroider for her a picture that said, "Love thy Neighbor." I said, "Yes I will. Where are you going to hang it?"

Mama answered, "Next door."

In reality, we are all foreigners. Most of the naturalized citizens came from parts of the world where persecution and tragedy drew a curtain of darkness over their lives. How often did they dream of freedom and the kind of life they found in America?

They had seen and experienced unspeakable abuse that destroyed the dignity of human beings, and yet, out of their dark despair they had the good fortune to come into the warmth and sunlight that was America. How truly the sages spoke when they said, "If there was no darkness, we would not appreciate the light."

When Papa's mother was ninety-four and his papa was dead, the boys sent money for Grandma to come to America to see her children again. Papa took me with him to Detroit for the reunion. I was the lucky one because the train was free if you were under six years old. Although I was six, I was carefully coached to say that I was five on the train. En route the conductor asked me how old I was. "I'm five on the train and six in school." The conductor was very kind. I don't know what Papa would have done if he had to pay for me, because I am sure he didn't have the fare.

# Chapter 8
# Five Oranges

"עס איז בעסער צו נעמען עסן אין מויל ווי וווייטיק אין האַרצן".

*"Es iz beser tsu nemen esn in moyl vi veytik in harts."*

"It is better to take food in the mouth rather than pain in the heart."

– Mama

There is a story Mama used to tell about the young widow with one child, who married an older widower with four children. In those days women did not work out of the home because they lacked the education and spoke very little English. She desperately needed a man to provide for her and her child. Just as troubled, the widower needed a woman to mother his children and care for them.

One day the new mother told the five children to sit down at the kitchen table. She had baked bread and placed one small, braided bread in front of each stepchild. Her child had none. She said, "See, I am not a wicked stepmother. I have given each of you a beautiful, fresh bread, but I have not given my own son any. Now you four children must show that you are not selfish by breaking your bread in half and giving that half to my son who has none." We were pretty smart kids, and we figured out pretty fast that her stepchildren each had half of a loaf of bread, while her son had two loaves of bread.

That story brings to mind another such scene. I don't remember ever having eaten an orange. I never remember seeing an orange in the house until one day Mama bought five oranges from the fruit peddler. Mama sat us around the kitchen table.

Papa, Sam, Izzy, Lil and I made five. There was no orange for Mama. Papa helped me start to peel the orange, and I watched my brothers and sister as they persevered in peeling their oranges. I copied them. Everyone broke their oranges apart in many sections. We put one section at a time into our mouths. As we bit down the sweet juice squirted out. It started to bother me as Mama busied herself around the kitchen. It never occurred to me to share my orange with Mama. Nobody else did. If she had wanted an orange she would have bought six.

Many times, in my adult life, I carried guilt because I did not share my orange with my mother. As I grew older, I realized something was very wrong with that picture. If Mama could afford only five oranges, she should have cut them into pieces and divided the five oranges into six portions. I finally admitted to myself that my mother had some "martyr" in her personality. If she had taken her share, I would not have had to go through life carrying the guilt of not sharing my orange. I finally had to admit that I was not a perfect person.

# Chapter 9
# The New Doll

"דו זאָלסט וואַקסן ווי אַ ציבעלע מיטן קאָפּ אין דער ערד."

*"Du zolst vaxn vi a tsibele mitn kop in der erd."*

"You should grow like an onion with your head in the ground."

– Mama

I never had a new doll. My Papa was a junk peddler and whenever he found a doll in the alley, he would bring it home to me, regardless of its condition. Mama cleaned it up for me. The eyes were supposed to open and close, but my dolls had eyes that were frozen open or closed. The wig was either gone or in a terrible mess, one leg was missing, or the hand was missing from the arm that was ready to fall off.

Papa told a dressmaker on his route that he had a seven-year-old girl that loved to dress dolls. He would appreciate it if she would save her scraps for me. It was just like *Chanukah* when she sent me a bundle of small, wonderful scraps of shiny pink satin, blue taffeta, white lace, thin white cotton for panties, light weight wool for a coat or jacket. I could hardly believe my eyes when I saw tiny buttons, blue and pink and green narrow ribbons, and even some elastic.

You could almost always find me on the front porch, sitting and sewing by hand. Every few minutes I ran into the house to have Mama thread the needle and tie a knot. She always made the thread double before she knotted it so that the thread would not slip out. If the doll was missing a leg, I would make a long skirt to hide the missing part. If the hand was gone, I made a pocket and stuck the arm into the pocket, then no one would know the doll was not perfect. I made a hat or tied a triangular piece of cloth on the head to hide the terrible wig. I used a beautiful ribbon to tie the hat on.

The Friedman family lived next door to the north of us. Every day their only daughter Shirley paraded in front of our house with her wonderful new wicker buggy. In the buggy was a white pillow at the bottom and a small fancy pillow at the head. There were two gorgeous new dolls in the buggy. The dolls had exquisite organdy outfits with matching socks and patent leather shoes. I was amazed at her possessions and thought they must be very rich.

One Friday afternoon close to my birthday, Mrs. Friedman and

Shirley came over to our house carrying a large cardboard box. Mrs. Friedman motioned to Shirley to give me the box. She hesitated but she did. I lifted the lid and saw the most wonderful doll I had ever seen. It was dressed in pink organdy with a matching bonnet trimmed with white lace, pink socks, a white-lace trimmed petticoat, panties, and black patent leather slippers. I told Shirley that her new doll was beautiful. Her mother said, "No, Jennie, this doll is a birthday gift to you because we know how much you love dolls. We know you will take good care of her."

I was speechless. Mama said, "Jennie, aren't you going to say thank you?" I jumped up, put the box down on the porch, then turned and hugged Mrs. Friedman and Shirley. I had tears in my eyes when I said thank you. Later, I went over and thanked Mr. Friedman because Mama explained that he earned the money they used to buy the doll.

The doll was much too precious to play with. I put the box and its unbelievable contents under Mama's bed. Every so often I would go into the bedroom, get down on my knees, pull the box out, lift the lid, and feast my eyes on my new treasure. I put the lid back on the box and shoved it back under the bed. I must have done this fifty times before I went happily to bed that night to dream of the incredible thing that happened to me that day.

It was summer and all the windows were open so I could hear Shirley screaming and crying all day long. I could hear her mother soothing her and telling her what a good thing their family had done. She reminded Shirley how many dolls she already had. The furor continued all day Saturday and all morning Sunday.

At lunchtime there was a knock on our door. Mama led a very sad-looking Mrs. Friedman into the kitchen where we all sat. Our nice neighbor said, "Mrs. Berger, I am so sorry, but my child is making herself sick. She has been screaming and crying since Friday, and I can't stand it anymore. I must ask for the doll back."

Mama said, "Jennie, go get the box from the bedroom." I walked slowly, with my chin on my chest trying my best not to cry. I pulled the box out from under the bed, but this time I did not lift the lid. I handed the gift to Mrs. Friedman. She looked very sad and again said how sorry she was.

So was I. Is it any wonder that I am a doll collector today?

# Chapter 10
# Sam

"הָאָב איך דיר נישט געלערנט רעספּעקט? דו מוזט רעספּעקטירן דעם געזעץ."

*"Hob ikh dir nisht gelernt respekt? du muzt respektirn dem gezets."*

"Haven't I taught you respect? You must respect the law."

— Papa

I was very lucky. Both of my brothers were loving and protective of me. On my eighth birthday, my brother Izzy gave me eight pennies and a large Hershey bar. That made me very happy. I tried to kiss him and say thank you, but he was at that awful age, and he said, "Get away from me." I embarrassed him.

When I was growing up it was extremely unusual for a Jewish boy to get in trouble with the law. In all of my young years, only two boys in our neighborhood went to prison. Frank Marks was sixteen years old and was influenced by a nineteen-year-old to drive the car in a robbery. His friend shot the store owner and killed him. Although Frank did not commit the robbery, he did not go into the store, he did not hold or shoot the gun, he was the getaway driver; therefore he was just as guilty as the shooter. Both boys were convicted and executed. My brother told me that Frank had to be buried outside the cemetery fence.

The second boy was fourteen years old and was influenced by a twenty-year-old to kidnap the grocer's son for ransom. The victim returned home safely, and no ransom money was paid but both boys went to prison because of the Lindbergh Law. The younger, the fourteen-year-old, went to the reformatory until he was eighteen and then transferred to the penitentiary. He was released at age twenty, for good behavior. He was a good citizen after his release.

None of us kids ever had money. We didn't even know what an allowance was. We got seven cents on Saturday. Five cents were for a ticket to the Palm Theater. Two cents were for two penny candies. I always bought two Tootsie Rolls. On Sunday we got a nickel for a double dip ice cream cone.

My oldest brother, Sam, was the first one to realize that he could get a job and earn some money. After he got a job, with his first paycheck he bought my mother a mirror for the living room wall. The second week he brought home a table lamp. A week before school started, Sam took me downtown and bought me six pairs of socks, six pairs of panties, and a slip. We rode the streetcar both ways. He accepted my kiss and hug, with a thank you.

Papa spoke to us at the supper table, "Children, there are three people to stay away from: a doctor, a lawyer, and a policeman. Sam, tell me, what kind of job do you have to buy your mother a mirror and a lamp, and to buy your sister underwear and socks, and nice clothes for yourself?" Sam finally admitted he was delivering whiskey for a bootlegger.

Papa went on to say, "Haven't I taught you respect? You must respect the law, and your job is against the law. Did you know that? You could go to jail. I have told all of you many times that you must respect your parents, each other, your teachers, policemen, and your elders. I know you want money that I cannot give you. I just don't have it. I will not break the law to get money. What would you all do if I went to jail? I work hard to bring home food, and to pay the rent, and get you the things you need. People may not admire what I do but it is honest, and I work hard."

"Sam, you must quit your job or you are not welcome in this house. You are setting a bad example for your brother and sisters. You make your mother cry because she worries about what could happen to you. Whatever happens to you, happens to all of us. Do you think your little sister would trade the underwear and socks for you to go to jail? Of course not."

Sam quit his job and got a corner downtown to sell newspapers. Every day he proudly gave Mama thirty-five cents. Sam then got his brother a corner to sell papers. Izzy also gave Mama thirty-five cents each day. The seventy cents made Mama's life better. The first thing she bought was Lilac Talcum Powder from the dime store because she loved to smell nice. She was proud of her boys and Papa told the boys that he had respect for them.

# Chapter 11
# Klansmen on the March

"The Ku Klux Klan is coming...*pogrom*."
– Papa

On the Sunday before Memorial Day, in 1926, small groups of neighbors gathered in front of the corner grocery and the Friedman's house. No one was smiling; there was none of the usual raucous laughter and backslapping. In the house, Mama and Papa spoke Russian back and forth, in hopes the children would not understand. We could tell our parents were nervous and worried.

"Is someone sick or dying?" I asked Mama.

"No, Jennie, everything is fine. Go play with your friends." I went outside and asked Sam and Izzy. They didn't know, yet both glanced nervously at the gathering neighbors. As children, we always assumed any trouble had to do with us because it usually did. I know my brothers were wondering what they had done and when the crowd down the street was going to head our way.

Lilly didn't know but she wouldn't even talk to me, her head buried in a book. "Go away," she snapped. "Can't you see I'm busy. If it's important, they'll tell us."

This left a lot of questions hanging. Who exactly were they – the neighbors – my parents – the police? Something was up – either something had happened or was going to happen.

I spent the day playing with my dolls in the front yard, watching the crowd down the street swell and diminish as different people came and went. Papa even joined the crowd and came back with a grim look on his face.

Dinner was quiet with Mama and Papa shooting glances back and forth. Explosive Russian erupted between my parents. It sounded like an argument but my parents never argued, at least not in front of us and certainly not at the dinner table. We cringed in our chairs giving each other troubled, questioning nudges. Whatever it was about, Papa won.

He turned to us, "Children, today we read in the paper that the Grand Dragon and his followers, the Ku Klux Klan, will march up West Colfax to Golden. They are coming through our neighborhood to scare us. We don't know what they plan to do, but we know they hate Jews."

"Who?" Lilly asked.

"A Grand Dragon?" I asked.

"The KKK," Papa said.

"A dragon?" I asked again.

"This is America," Sam said with authority. "The KKK can't hurt us."

Mama shot Sam a dark look. "The paper says there will be five hundred of them," Papa darkly informed Sam. "Who can say what a crowd like that will do? And, if they do something evil, who can stop them?"

Sam tried to reason, "The police for one –"

"The police!" Mama argued. "How many police are going to be there, two?"

"What kind of dragon will it be?" I asked. "Like a big lizard?"

Papa said one word, "*Pogrom.*"

Silence engulfed the table. We knew what a *pogrom* was. Our parents had told us about that plenty of times; it was the reason they had come to America. "This isn't Russia," Sam told us. "We have rights and freedom here in America, and *pogroms* don't happen in this country."

Papa beat his fist on the table, and we all jumped. Angrily he turned on Sam, "Fine, so you say this is America! I say you stay away from them! And that goes for the rest of you!"

Papa left the table, scraping his chair on the floor. He stomped out the front door to go down the block to talk with the group of men still gathered there.

"I wonder if this dragon has wings?" I mused.

After dinner, the neighborhood children started gathering like the adults. The KKK was the main topic at everyone's dinner table. Sam, being the oldest, was the ringleader as we milled around him.

Bennie was appointed as lookout in case any adult got close enough to overhear our worried whisperings.

"They will march only a few blocks from here," Sam said. "We could sneak over and have a quick peek. No one will know."

Izzy nervously chewed his finger. "OK," he finally agreed.

"I'm not going," Lilly said. "Papa told us not to." We had been forbidden to go but it wouldn't be the first time we had disobeyed our parents.

"Stay here and be a chicken then, we don't care," Sam said and gestured around the group, showing that the rest of us were very brave.

We tried to look brave as we pictured the punishment that was in store for us. "I'm not a chicken!" Lilly snapped back.

"I'm going," Harry Schreiber said.

"Be stupid then," Lilly snarled, "and your father will beat you again."

"I don't want another beating," Dave said. "Maybe I won't go either."

Sam looked at the crowd with disgust. "All of you are chickens! I'm going, and so is Izzy."

"Me, too!" I piped up. I wasn't about to miss a dragon.

The following day dawned clear with a brilliant blue sky. Every child was outside in his front yard or playing softball in the street. It was almost as if the scary feelings of yesterday were gone.

Where the adults were at, I didn't know, inside hiding, perhaps, reliving the horrific past of Russia and the *pogroms.*

The streets slowly emptied of children. The one lie that each of us told was that we were going to play at someone else's house that day. I saw Sam and Izzy sauntering off down the street and quickly followed them. Lilly was sitting on the stoop, reading, and wouldn't look up from her book.

My brothers and I gathered with the rest of the neighborhood children behind the huge billboard on Colfax and Hazel Court. The sign started about two feet off the ground, and if we lay on our stomachs, we could peek out from underneath it. We felt this hiding place offered plenty of protection since we couldn't just sit on the curb.

Colfax Avenue, a main street, was empty of cars and people and strangely quiet. We nervously spoke in hushed whispers as we waited as our excitement mounted by the minute. Nothing happened.

Against Sam's orders, Izzy kept sneaking out from behind the billboard and running into the street, looking off into the distance for the parade. Sam was worried an adult would see Izzy and report his whereabouts to our parents.

We waited, and still nothing happened. A few kids were beginning to wonder whether the parade was going to take place at all.

"I'm getting hot," Benny announced.

"I'm thirsty," I complained.

"I don't think they're coming," Dave told Sam.

"Quiet!" Sam whispered loudly. "Go home if you want, I'm staying for the parade. Izzy, go check the street again."

The hot early summer sun beat down, but nobody left. We had been lying on our stomachs, but now just about everybody was up doing something. The boys were punching each other in the arm. An unplanned game of kick ball had started. Another group of children played rock-scissors-paper.

I patiently waited by Sam's side – I wasn't going to miss the dragon. We heard a noise that sounded like a heartbeat – drums in the distance. Izzy ran back and announced the parade was finally coming. Everyone quickly quit goofing off and settled down on his or her stomach underneath the billboard; we were ready for the show.

They looked like ghosts, dressed up for Halloween, with long white sheets thrown over their bodies. The headgear was even weirder. Everyone wore pointed hoods that hid their faces with two holes for eyes and one hole for a mouth. The leader wore a purple satin cape, lined with yellow over his white sheet, and to complete the outfit, a purple hood to match. His cane kept time with the drummers who followed him, and then behind them were about five hundred of those ghosts followed, marching slowly in time. There wasn't a dragon in sight.

The parade lasted for quite some time. They marched and we watched. Next to me there was a commotion. I looked over to see Ted, a good friend of Sam's, restraining Sam's arm. "Don't be stupid." Ted told him in a hushed whisper. "Throwing rocks at the KKK could get us in big trouble."

Sam grinned maniacally. "Look at those idiots; they look like they're going to a Halloween party!"

"Put down the rock!" Ted insisted. "Our parents will definitely find out we were here if you start throwing stuff." As if they heard us, the entire parade came to a complete halt. We all held our breath. I looked nervously from Sam to the KKK members and then back to Sam. What would happen to us now? And where was that dragon?

After what seemed like an eternity, the parade started again. Twice more the assembly came to a complete halt, and the only sound filling the air was a constant drumbeat. It took about half an hour for the entire parade to pass. I kept waiting for the dragon to appear. I knew what the giant lizard should look like – tall, a wing span of at least a block, green scales, flashing red eyes, and maybe breathing fire.

The last of the sheets fluttered out and we couldn't hear the drum beat anymore. All in all, I was very disappointed – no dragon. We quickly scattered, each one hoping our parents hadn't missed us. Sam slung his arm around my shoulders and told Izzy he was proud of us. We had seen the dreaded KKK and nothing had happened.

"Why do they wear those sheets?" Izzy asked.

"So no one will know who they are," Sam replied.

"That's dumb," Izzy said. "Why would you want to be in a parade and not have anyone know who you are?"

"They didn't have a dragon," I complained.

Sam laughed, "Jennie, the guy wearing the purple cape at the head of the parade is called the Grand Dragon." I still didn't understand.

Papa was waiting on the steps when we rounded the corner. He didn't look very happy. Sam's grip on my shoulder tightened, and I felt my stomach go into knots. We were in trouble now. We slowly approached Papa. Feeling the tension in the air, Lilly looked up from her book to see what was going on. "So, you went to the parade," Papa said. It wasn't a question; it was a statement. Sam nodded. Izzy intently studied a piece of grass that had caught his attention. "I told you not to go," Papa said.

"They couldn't hurt us," Sam replied defiantly. "I told you, this is America; we have rights as citizens, and we're protected by laws!"

To Papa this spiel was beginning to sound like a broken record. There were plenty of rumors going around about what was still happening in Mississippi that involved the KKK, and if those things were happening there, they could be happening here. "I'm very disappointed in both of you," Papa told Sam and Izzy. "And to take a child along," Papa gestured at me, "was very wrong. You weren't thinking at all."

"I went to see the dragon," I said, "'but they didn't have one.'"

Papa stared at me, trying to understand what I was babbling about. He slowly shook his head. "Don't ever pull a foolish stunt like that again." Mama talked to Papa through the screen door, something in Russian. He answered, gave all of us one final glare, and went inside.

"He should have whipped each of you till you couldn't sit down," Lilly said, telling the punishment that we felt was coming. Sam scowled at her and then drifted off to visit with his friends to see what their parents had done. Children were playing kick ball in the street, and Izzy went to join them. I stayed with Lilly and played alone with my dollies. Why Papa didn't punish us, I don't know. I think he was just relieved that we returned home safely. I know that part of him wanted to believe that we were safe in America, and if his children could watch a KKK rally and not get harmed, maybe we were.

You're never wrong doing the right thing!

# Chapter 12
# The Snowstorm

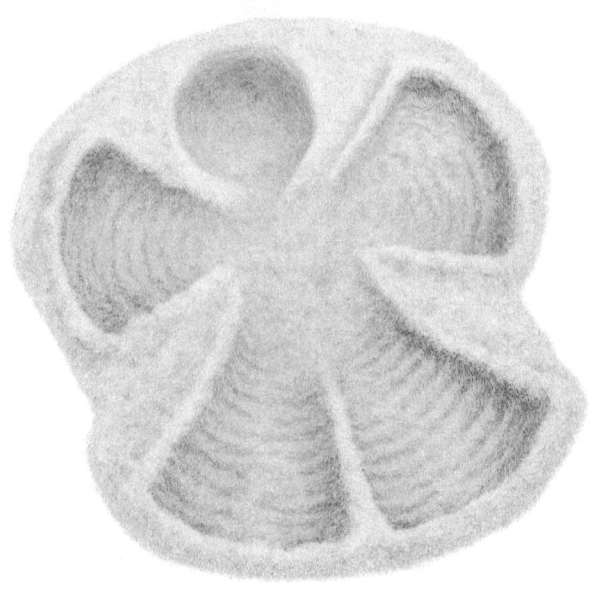

"Jennie, ve are millionaires."
– Mama

I was ten years old and was fascinated with the frost on the window. I fell asleep watching the large snowflakes falling through the moonlight. I dreamed about streets and houses buried under the snow. When I awoke, I leaped out of bed to see what had happened during the night. The window was completely covered with heavy, squiggle frost. I couldn't see through the frost, so I melted a see-through spot by pressing my warm hand on the glass. I saw that it was still snowing and everything looked exactly as I dreamed it would.

The only warm room in the house was the kitchen heated by the wood and coal stove. I was shivering so I dressed as fast as I could. First, I pulled on the long black stockings that Mama had laid out for me. Mama had knitted a sleeveless, low-necked jumper out of all colored scraps of yarn, sort of like Joseph's coat. On cold days I wore it under my dress. It was perfect for a day like today. I pulled my dress on, put on my galoshes and grabbed the rest of the things Mama had laid out – my mittens, stocking hat, and my winter coat – and dashed into the kitchen. I dropped the outside clothes in the corner, sat down at the kitchen table, and started to eat the hot oatmeal. It was too hot so I had to blow on every spoonful so I could get out into the snow faster. I emptied the bowl, put on my coat, hat and mittens, and ran out the front door. I stopped short on the front porch – the steps were gone! The street was gone, and the sky had disappeared too.

Somehow, I slid down the three steps that were not there. The bushes and trees were all round balls. There was not a single foot-step in the snow. I struggled through the hip high snow and was breathless before I managed twenty feet. I stopped to rest and looked around. Oh boy! It was perfect to make an angel.

I fell backwards, stiff-legged with my arms hugging my body. I swept the snow with my stiff arms, from thighs out and around, up past my shoulders. Then I traced the same pattern down, then back up and then down again. I stood up to admire my artistic endeavor.

There was a perfect angel, wings and all. I hoped no one would spoil it because I wanted to admire it again on my way home from school. I was now breathless again from the struggle through the deep snow. By the time I reached the school yard I was feeling guilty because I had messed up the perfect snow. The boys were jumping in and out of the snowbanks. I wanted to jump with them, but I would be the only girl. So, I went up the shoveled steps and went into the warm hall. All day long the teacher watched the snow with a worried look on her face.

When the three o'clock bell rang, we all jumped up eagerly to get our wraps on so we could play in the snow. The smaller children were gathered at the exit door with their teacher. They were waiting for their parents, bewildered, and worried, until they spotted their mamas or papas. I dashed through the door and out into the wonderful, soft snow. I took the same route home that I had taken to school so that I could visit my angel. Oh heck! It was all covered with new snow and the beautiful angel was gone. I made a new angel and hurried home because I was getting cold feet and hands.

Mama was waiting at the door to help me off with my wet clothes. She opened the oven door and pushed a chair up to the stove. She wrapped my legs in a blanket, plopped me into the chair, and put my stiff legs on the oven door. Then she gave me a hot baked apple wrapped in newspaper so I could hold it without burning my hands. By someone else's standards we were poor. Mama leaned down and gave me a sloppy wet kiss on my cold cheek and said, "Jennie, ve are millionaires."

# Chapter 13
# The Wedding

"װען אַ נאַר איז שטיל, װײַסן מענטשן נישט צי ער איז אַ נאַר אָדער אַ חכם."

*"Ven a nar iz shtil, veysn mentshn nisht tsi er iz a nar oder a khkhm."*

"When a fool is quiet, people don't know if he's a fool or a sage."

— Mama

Papa and Mama were both forty-one years old. My oldest brother, Sam, was twenty, Izzy was eighteen, my sister Lil was sixteen and I was twelve. We were all dressed in our best clothes for a Jewish wedding in the synagogue. In those days the men and women did not sit together so that the men would not be distracted from their prayers. In some synagogues the room had a divider and the women sat in the rear behind a curtain. In our shul, the women sat on a small balcony at the back of the chapel. Lil and I sat upstairs with Mama, and my brothers sat downstairs with Papa.

A female voice was singing, "Here comes the bride" as the lovely bride came down the center aisle. At the end of the ceremony, the groom smashed a glass with his shoe, and everyone clapped and yelled, "*Mazel tov!*"

We all went down to the basement where the tables were laden with herring, *ayer kichel*, honey cake, *mandel broyt*, strudel, and large bowls of fruit. There were wash tubs with ice for the bottles of pop for the children and the women. The men were all crowded around a table where the *schnapps* was flowing generously. Children were running wild in circles. The men became boisterous with laughter and spicy jokes. The women sat along the wall talking to each other. The young girls were in one group and the young men stood together in another corner. After everyone had their fill, the band started to play *"Cho'sen Kaleh Mazel Tov."* The boys asked the girls to dance, and my brother Sam was the best dancer on the floor. Mama and I were proud of him.

By this time the men had too much schnapps, and each one started to see himself as the young stud he was twenty years earlier. They were joking and flirting with the young girls who were completely repelled by the lechers. Hershel Klein was the worst. He was short and overweight with most of the fat on his stomach. His face was red and sweaty. He had his arm around the shoulder of a seventeen-year-old who was squirming to get away from him. The man was obnoxious. Papa looked at Hershel and then at Mama and smiled. Mama leaned over to her friend, and I heard her say, "Thank G-d that isn't my fool."

# Chapter 14
# The Talker

"It's not enough to just be good. You must be good for something."
— Anonymous

I was a child who did not misbehave. I showed respect to everyone and knew my place. Mama told me I was her only child that never gave her a moment of trouble, but I did have one problem. When I got excited or enthusiastic, I could not contain myself. I interrupted and I talked. The teachers did not know what to do with me.

My problem started in kindergarten and followed me through my school years. In kindergarten the teacher washed my mouth with soap, put tape over my mouth, and put me out in the hall for a full hour. Do you have any idea how long an hour is when you are five years old?

When I was an adult I ran into Mrs. Balaban, who was my kindergarten teacher. I asked her what I could have said at five years old that would call for such severe punishment. She laughed and told me, "It's not what you said; you just would not shut up for a minute."

In the fourth grade, Mrs. Auger called me up to her desk and told me that the principal wanted to talk to me. She handed me a hall pass. I asked if I could go to the toilet first because I was scared. As I sat in the outer office, I saw a man and his son leaving the principal's office. The father held the crying boy by his collar. This sight didn't help at all. Mr. Kluxton, the principal, stood in his doorway and summoned me in with the crook of his finger. He motioned for me to sit down in the chair in front of his desk. "How are you, Jennie?"

"Did I do something bad? Am I in trouble?"

The principal smiled and assured me I was not in trouble. He said, "I need someone who can talk well. Mrs. Auger tells me you can talk, and talk, and talk. Would you be willing to give the students a message from me? I have it all written out for you. You can take it home and study it tonight. Be ready to do this tomorrow morning."

Mama got my best clothes pressed and laid out. She put Vaseline on my patent leather sandals so they would shine and look new. I was very proud, and I practiced in front of the whole family that night. They all thought I did a good job but suggested I should end on a strong note. "Say it like you mean business." I was to go to every room, starting with my fourth-grade room. The teacher told the class that Mr. Kluxton had asked me to make an announcement, as she called me to the front of the room.

I started, "Mr. Kluxton wanted me to tell all of you that they have planted grass and flowers so that we could be proud of our school and enjoy the beauty. I was made a monitor to make an announcement and to tell all of you 'TO STAY OFF THE GRASS!' "

I was President of the eighth grade, junior high school class. One day, Miss London, our English teacher, lost patience with me. "Jennie Berger, I would enjoy going on a picnic with you, but I cannot stand you in class another day. Your clowning around and constant talking disrupts the class. The only thing that runs right in your head is your mouth. You gather your books and go to Study Hall right now." As I was walking out of the room, Harry Guber stood up and swept his arm toward me and said, "The pride of the 8A class."

In high school I had the female lead in every class play. Years later, when I was fifty years old, I won an International Speech Contest for the Toastmistress Organization. Imagine winning first place over forty thousand women!

During World War II, I was Mistress of Ceremonies for the Malloy Varieties. We played at army base hospitals and the USO.

Later I wrote a one woman show and performed it at the AT&T Christmas party and the Air Force Academy's big annual banquet. I was hired to do my show at conventions at the Broadmoor and the Antler's Hotel in Colorado Springs, *Bar Mitzvahs,* wedding rehearsal dinners, and fund-raising affairs for large corporations. The money I earned helped my grandson pay for medical school. I did ten free shows a year for nursing homes and rehabilitation centers.

As the years passed my memory started to slip so I worked with a book in front of me. No one seemed to mind the book, even on cruises. I did eleven minutes at my grandson's wedding, and they rolled on the floor.

Sooo – now my eyesight just doesn't do the job if the light isn't perfect. I'm afraid my heyday is over. Oh well, it was great while it lasted. My one wish is to find a way to tell my kindergarten teacher, Mrs. Augher, Mr. Kluxton, and Mrs. London, that my talking was not all bad.

# Chapter 15
# Friendship

"עֶר זאָל פֿאַרלירן אַלע זײַנע צײן, אַחוץ אײַנס, און יענע זאָל שטענדיק וויי טאָן."

*"Er zol farlirn ale zeyne tseyn akhuts eyn, aun yene zol shtendik vey ton."*

"He should lose all his teeth, save one, and that one should always hurt."

– *Bubbe*

The very first class was called Cooking Class. My partner was Helen Turner, from Barnum. We sat together at a small table just big enough for two chairs. We could have been sisters or twins because we both had light brown hair, blue-green eyes, and light skin. The only difference was Helen wore a Buster Brown haircut that looked like her mother had put a bowl on her head to cut it. I stopped wearing the Buster Brown cut two years earlier. Now I put my hair up in rags to get the curl. We were both five feet tall and neither one of us had the best clothes, although we were always clean and neat.

Helen wore long underwear and wore her black cotton stockings high on her legs. I wore my famous "Hungarian Flour Mills Sack Bloomers" and when I left home my black stockings were high on my legs. When I turned the corner, the stockings were rolled down below my knees. Before I turned that corner after school, the stockings went back up high on my legs. I had lots of friends, but Helen followed me around like a little lost soul. She asked me if she could share my locker and I felt sorry for her and said, "OK." We became fast friends. She told me she didn't ever remember laughing until she met me. Her eyes were so sad and she was afraid of her shadow. She was so afraid of her mother's wrath that she wouldn't even whisper in school. Helen could not take a chance of getting in trouble.

Our first cooking lesson was on the proper way to prepare vegetables, so they were not under or overcooked. We made carrots and peas. I told Helen I had never mixed 'parrots and keys' before. We both cracked up at my mistake and started giggling. We fed on each other's laughter and pretty soon we couldn't stop. Before we knew what happened we were both in the principal's office.

Mr. Kluxton, the principal, was a very serious man, or so we thought. "Girls, tell me what happened." Helen was scared and struck dumb, so I talked. "Mr. Kluxton, I made a mistake and said, 'parrots and keys' instead of carrots and peas and it made me laugh and we couldn't stop giggling. Honest, we tried but we couldn't stop."

We started to giggle all over again and he was laughing with us. When we three finally settled down he told us to go into the restroom and wash our faces with cold water, get a drink of water and go back to class. "Do not go into that room if you are still giggling. Just sit on the floor outside the classroom door until you can act like two young ladies."

Helen was also in my English class, and I sat near her, and we whispered and passed notes. Miss London, our teacher, was an old maid and wore the same dark green dress every day for the three years I went to that school. One day she became very angry at Helen and me. I told her it was not Helen's fault, that I was the one who talked and laughed first. Miss London said, "You will go to the Study Hall for the rest of the semester, and you will fail English."

I can still see the disappointment in my father's eyes when I brought home the report card showing I failed English. He told me he knew I was smarter than that, so I told him what happened. I saw him glance at Mama and get that funny half-smile. He tried to act stern and said, "This had better never happen again."

One day in class, Helen leaned over to me and said, "Show me a Jew. I want to see what a Jew looks like."

"I am a Jew, Helen."

"You can't be a Jew; you look like everybody else."

"What did you expect, horns or an eagle-beak nose?"

"Wait until I go home and tell my mother that a Jew looks just like me. I know she won't believe me."

We walked together when we headed home from school, until we reached Colfax Avenue, then she went her way and I went mine. One day I invited her to come home with me. "My Mama always has baked apples waiting after school."

"I would love to go to your house, but I have too many chores to do before my mother gets home from work. If they are not done, she gets real mean. Why don't you come home with me? If you help me, I can get the chores done fast and we can play Xs and Os for a while."

"I can't today because I didn't ask my mother. If I get permission I will go home with you tomorrow."

Mama said it was OK, but to be home before dark.

When we got to Helen's house there was a man in the living room. She didn't introduce him to me. "Is that your father?" I whispered.

"No."

"Is he your uncle?"

"No."

"Who is he, then?"

"He just lives with us."

I swept the porch and the steps while Helen washed the breakfast dishes and set the table for dinner. We got on opposite sides of the bed and made it up in a hurry. Then we peeled six potatoes and put them on the coal stove to boil. We were free to play Xs and Os. I left at five o'clock because the sun was setting. I didn't get to meet Helen's mean mother.

One beautiful spring day Helen came to school with red, swollen eyes. "Helen, have you been crying? Did your mother hit you?"

"I tried to make myself oatmeal for breakfast and I didn't read the instructions like I should have. I put the entire box of oatmeal in the boiling water. It boiled over the pot onto the stove, over the stove edge, and down on the floor. It just never quit. I grabbed the pot with a towel and dumped it into the sink. It splashed on the floor as I walked. I tried to clean it up but there was so much oatmeal, and it was so slimy I couldn't get it done or I would have been late for school. I don't know what I am going to do. My mother will kill me."

We ran all the way home to my house and told my mother what

had happened to Helen. Mama asked "Helen, do you have a dustpan and a pail?"

"Yes, ma'am."

"Jennie, you take this pail and dustpan and these rags and go help Helen clean up. But girls do not put the oatmeal in the sink or tub because it will stop up the plumbing. Carry it out to the ash pit by the alley."

By this time Helen was sobbing because she had already dumped the oatmeal in the sink and her mother would kill her. Mama put her apron on and said, "Girls, let's go." We must have been a funny sight. Helen was leading the way at top speed carrying the rags. Then came Mama carrying the pail. I was the cow's tail marching behind them with the dustpan swinging as I went.

When we stepped into Helen's house, we peeked into the kitchen from the front room. We couldn't believe our eyes. Oatmeal was everywhere, covering the top of the stove, running down onto the floor. It was splashed onto the woodwork and the wall where Helen had tried to clean in a hurry that morning. Mama rolled up her sleeves and told us to take off our shoes and socks because that would be one less thing to clean. We lined up our shoes and socks in the front room and were very careful not to slip as we went into the kitchen. The first thing Mama did was scoop up the oatmeal in the sink into the pot and carried it out to the ash pit. She pulled the garden hose to the back fence and rinsed the gunk out of the pot and off her feet. She came back in and told us to tuck our skirts into the elastic of our panty legs and to get down on our hands and knees and scoop up whatever we could with the dustpan into the pails. "Take the pails and the dustpan out to the alley and wash them off with the hose. Then, you come back in and start again until you have it all up."

We could not believe how much oatmeal a full box of Quaker's could make. I think we made twenty trips out to the alley, hosing down our icky feet and washing the dust pans and the pails for the next trip. Finally, it was all scooped up. By this time Mama had cleaned the pot and the sink and the stove. We filled the pails with soapy water and started to wash down the walls, the woodwork, and the door. At five minutes to five we were finally done with the kitchen. All three of us dashed around making beds, setting the table, and peeling potatoes. Mama and I put on our shoes and socks. Mama said for Helen to wash her face and comb her hair. We grabbed our rags, pail and dustpan, and left by the back door, out the back yard, and down the alley. It was now five twenty-five. Helen had five minutes to spare before her mother got home.

Mama and I held hands as we hurried home. She said, "It feels good to help a friend, doesn't it?"

Papa beat us home that day and was surprised to see that nothing was cooking and the table wasn't set. He walked through the house calling Mama's name. He was worried. This was the very first time he had come home to an empty house. My brothers and sister walked in, and Papa asked if they knew where Mama was. They didn't. Just then we walked in. You could see the relief in everyone's eyes. Papa smiled and pretended to be angry. He made a fist and pounded on the kitchen table, "Supper must be on the table at six o'clock."

The older kids and Mama burst into laughter. I didn't think it was that funny. Papa said when I was a little older, he would explain why it was funny. I nagged my brother Izzy until he explained the joke.

It seems that Mr. Yopolsky had a house rule that he emphasized by making a fist and pounding the table, "Supper must be on the table at six o'clock." One day Yopolsky came home from work and there was no supper on the table. He walked into the bedroom and found his wife in bed with the neighbor. He made a fist and pounded on the dresser, "I come home from work and find my wife in bed with another man and there is no supper on the table. SUPPER MUST BE ON THE TABLE AT SIX O'CLOCK!"

One day we were walking home from school and Helen stopped in her tracks. "Can you keep a secret?"

"Well, it's hard for me. You know I talk a lot and could blurt it out by mistake."

"Oh, dear," Helen said as her eyes filled with tears.

"But, if you tell me not to repeat the secret and if I swear on my mother's honor, then I would never tell it."

"OK, I trust you. When I am through with eighth grade next month, I am going to try to go to my brother in California. I have been saving my babysitting money. I need eighteen dollars for the bus fare, and I already have sixteen dollars and twenty-five cents. I am going to write a letter to my brother and ask him if I can come to California and live with him. I would get a job too. The law says I can work after the eighth grade."

"Why do you want to leave? Don't you want to finish school?"

"I hate Tom and I'm afraid of him."

"Does he hit you?" "No, but I hate him, and I can't tell my mother because she will be mad at me. Anyway, Tom and my mother get drunk every night and my mother's very mean when she drinks. I just can't live with them anymore."

"OK Helen, I will keep your secret."

"That's only part of the secret. I want my brother to answer my letter at your house, so my mother won't find out. Do you think it will be OK with your mother if he mails the answer to your house?"

When I talked to Mama about it, she said she would talk it over with Papa because it isn't a good idea to keep secrets from your parents. I saw Mama talking to Papa on the summer porch. After supper Papa asked me to sit down and talk to him. "Who is Tom? Is he married to Helen's mother?"

"No. Is he her uncle?"

"No."

"Is he a boarder? Does he pay to live there in a separate room?"

"I don't think so. There are only two bedrooms. One is Helen's and one is her mother's."

"What does Helen call him?"

"She told me she doesn't know what to call him, so she just calls him Tom."

"Jennie, I don't think you should go to Helen's house anymore. Let Helen come here to play when she can. I hate to take any pleasure away from her because it doesn't sound like she has such a good life. I have to insist that you don't go there. You can still be her friend at school, and you can still walk home with her. You tell her that I said it is all right for her brother to write a letter to her at our address."

I told Helen the good news about the letter first, and then the bad news about what Papa said about going to her house. Helen understood. A week had passed after her letter was mailed. We ran home from school every night to see if the answer was there. Finally, after the eleventh day, as we approached my house, we saw Mama on the porch waving a white envelope in the air. Helen opened the envelope, but she couldn't read the letter for the tears in her eyes, so I read it aloud. I also saw a five-dollar bill in the envelope.

Her brother said he understood the problem and he would be happy for Helen to come to live with him. He already had a waitress job lined up for her at the diner where he ate often. With the five dollars Helen had enough for the bus fare and a little left over for a meal. She didn't have a suitcase, so Mama told her to go to the grocery store and get a cardboard box. We had a piece of rope to make a handle. Helen left the box at our house and brought a few things over every day. She left four days after school ended.

Mama packed her a lunch to save her money – four pumpernickel-and-salami sandwiches and six apples.

Papa and I took her to the bus station in the horse and wagon. I went in with her and Papa helped her buy the ticket and get on the bus. We hugged and cried and vowed to write to each other at least once a month. I said I would someday come to see her in California.

Helen and I didn't write every month, but we did correspond for many years. She was married twice and divorced twice. She never failed to tell me in her letter that I was the one bright spot in her life. The last letter I mailed to her when we were sixty-five years old was returned unopened and stamped DECEASED.

## Chapter 16
# Come Back

"…you shall love your fellow as yourself."
– Leviticus 19:18

Mama came into the house in a hurry, washed her hands quickly, grabbed a pot, filled it with water and placed it on the stove. She then started peeling potatoes, mumbling to herself, "I hope they will be done in time for supper."

I asked, "Mama, where have you been? You are always home at this time."

Mama answered, "I went down to say hello to the new neighbor that bought Stein's house. She moved in on Monday."

"Do you like her? Is she nice?"

Mama sighed. "Yes, she's nice, but I couldn't get away from her. I didn't have so much time – I told her I was her neighbor – I didn't coffee *klatch*, but I wanted her to know if she needed somebody, I was her friend. Anything I could do to help her – just ask. We talked for a while and then I got up to leave, and she said, 'Come back.' So, I sat back down, and we talked some more. Who her neighbors were – what they did for a living – something about the children. And then I stood up to go. When I got to the door again, she said, 'Come back.' I couldn't insult her or hurt her feelings, so I went back, and we talked some more. She must have been lonesome.

"After a while it was getting late and I told her I really have to leave. Again, she said, 'Come back,' but this time I said, 'I'm sorry, I have to go home and start supper,' and I left."

I said, "Oh, Mama, she must have thought – how do I get rid of this lady? She meant, 'Come back again.' You will have to explain to her that you are not a pest – that you misunderstood."

Mama said sarcastically, "How much money would it cost her to say, 'Come back again'?"

# Chapter 17
# Bubbe's Football

"װייל פון א קינד איז שײן אלעס."

"...veyl fun a kind iz sheyn ales."

"...because from a child is beautiful anytink."

— *Bubbe*

I n 1925, when I was 7 years old, Mama's mother was brought over from Russia to live with us. *Bubbe* was 71 and there was something wrong with her hips. She walked funny and *oykit* most of the time. Today it's the fashion to put old *bubbes* in the nursing home, but I loved having my *Bubbe* in the house because she thought everything I said and everything I did was "byureful." Whenever I gave her a picture it went up on the wall, like a Rembrandt. I remember that Mama always smelled nice, perfumed with lilac talcum from the dime store and I liked that. But *Bubbe* smelled good too. She smelled like honey cake, *mandel broyt*, and chicken soup. If I guessed what was cooking, I got a sample.

I came in from playing one day and found the house torn apart for the real spring cleaning before Passover. *Bubbe* and Mama wore scarves on their heads to protect their clean hair. The white lace curtains were taken down, washed, and starched. The windows were washed, and the curtains were rehung. All the furniture was polished, and the floors were waxed. The rugs were hung on the clothesline, and my brothers were beating the dust out of them.

The leaves were put into the dining room table until it was big enough for 12 people. All the dishes were odd pieces and hardly any matched. The glasses were everything from tin cups and Mason jars to yahrzeit and jelly glasses. The silverware wasn't too bad, because Mama had borrowed from a neighbor. There was an ironing board resting on an apple box at each end, long enough to hold four small children.

I thought the table looked great, but I heard *Bubbe* say she needed a football for the center of the table. I couldn't imagine what on earth she needed a football for. I was pretty sure she wasn't going to play with it, but that didn't matter. A football was my department. If I could get my hands on one, I would be doing my part to make the big party a success. Everyone would be proud of me and I would be important.

I went to work. Benny Eisen wasn't home. Harry Gotlieb wouldn't give up his football for any kind of deal I offered – he wouldn't trade or sell. I hated to go to Sam Wiener, but he was the only one left who had a football. Besides, I knew he didn't like girls. I took a chance and, just as I expected, he pushed me down. I was persistent and he finally agreed to trade for my sled and bag of marbles.

I took my precious football to the filling station and the man filled it with air until it was really hard. I then went home and polished it until it shone. I put it in the middle of the dining room table and waited for someone to notice and be proud of me.

I heard Mama yelling at the top of her voice, "Jennie, you know *Bubbe* is having a party. Can't you put your toys where they belong?"

"But it's not mine, it's for *Bubbe*. She said she wanted a football for the middle of the table."

Mama started to laugh and said, "Don't you even understand your *Bubbe* when she talks?"

I ran out to the back porch and started to cry, that awful sobbing that is almost like hiccups and your breath comes in little jerks, and your chest hurts, and you just can't stop crying. I was still trying to stop when the company came. I was sad and very quiet even though they gave me two matzo balls instead of my usual one.

After supper *Bubbe* was proudly walking around from person to person offering fruit from the most beautiful cut glass bowl I ever saw. In it were oranges, apples, peaches, grapes, cherries, plums, and bananas and in the center was Sam Weiner's football. Uncle Sol offered *Bubbe* a compliment. "Esther, dots de most beautiful football I ever sawd."

*Bubbe* looked at him with much superiority and coached Uncle Sol, "So lisnet, Sol, and you vil loin somtink. Dis cut gless is a frutball and dis in the middle is a football."

"Very smot, Esther, so tell me somtink. Vy you got de football in de frutball?"

"Becaws today my Jenele brought me a nize present, dis football. It's beautiful NO? It's beautiful YES, because from a child is beautiful anytink."

Everyday above the ground is a good one.

# Chapter 18
# Mother's Day

"אזוי לאַנג ווי דו ביסט געזונט, קענסטו זיין צופרידן."

*"Azoy lang vi du bist gezunt, kenstu zeyn tsufridn."*

"So long as you're healthy, you can be happy."

– Molly Picon

As the sun set on Friday night, the Sabbath began. Mama lit the candles and said the blessing. All of us listened intently, hoping for a clue as to what she might want or need. Sunday was Mother's Day, and we were at a loss as to what to get for that special woman in our lives. As usual, Mama never asked for anything for herself. Instead, she asked for good health for Papa and her children, and that the next week should be no worse than the last.

This year would be different; we could actually afford to buy Mama something for Mother's Day. Sam and Izzy sold papers. Lilly and I earned money ripping linings from the woolen coats for Papa.

After dinner, we secretly met in the alley at the back of the house, deciding what we should get Mama. A new broom? A new pan? A new apron? A box of powder from the dime store? Sam knew where to get a dozen roses for one dollar. We finally decided a dozen red roses would be perfect. We each gave Sam 25 cents, and that was enough since there was no sales tax at that time.

The next day Izzy, Lilly, and I greeted Sam as soon as he arrived home after work; the roses were wrapped in green wax paper and carefully tucked under his arm. Lilly took the flowers from him as though she were handling a newborn. I went in and got Mama to come out.

We stood on the front porch, a half circle around Mama. Lilly presented the long, green wax paper package. "An vat is dis?" Mama asked.

We all yelled, "Happy Mother's Day!" She delicately peeled back the paper and exposed the heads of the roses. "Oh! I love roses!" She was touched by the wonderful gift; instead of buying something practical, or useful, this was a gift of the soul. Tears came to her eyes as she buried her nose in the heads of the roses and breathed deeply. In turn, Mama hugged and kissed each one of us. We followed her into the house. Mama murmured all the way into the kitchen, "Just look at them! I never dreamt I'd have so many."

She gently laid the roses on the kitchen table and unwrapped the wax paper, which she carefully folded and set aside. Reaching up high on a shelf she got the old glass pitcher with the broken handle. She had saved many green stamps to get that pitcher. The handle had been broken for a long time, but she wouldn't, couldn't, throw the pitcher away. After filling it with water, she placed the roses in the pitcher, but only after smelling each individual one and exclaiming, "Ahhh!" Three delicate ferns had also been added to the package and Mama arranged them among the roses.

We all stood back and admired the large red roses filling the pitcher. This was something none of us had seen before. Oh, sure, there had been flowers on the table before, lovely flowers from the garden. but never anything like this. Mama kissed each one of us again.

Mama left the kitchen to wash her face and comb her hair. She also put on a clean house dress since it was an important occasion. When she returned, she placed the pitcher of roses on the dining room table and admired them again. "No one should have this much beauty to themselves," she whispered.

"But you deserve them, Mama," I protested.

Mama gave me the knowing eye; it was the look that meant I didn't understand, but hopefully, one day I would. "Beauty is to be shared," she said. Mama removed three roses from the pitcher, along with one piece of fern and loosely wrapped them up in the green wax paper. She handed the package to me. "Jennie, take these down the block to the widow who lives next to the corner store. Tell Mrs. Weiss 'Happy Mother's Day' from the Berger family."

I looked at the roses in my arms and then at the remaining roses in the pitcher. "Do you see?" Mama said as she pointed to the roses on the table. "There are so many you don't notice that any are missing. And the joy is doubled by giving away a little of what you have."

She was right; you had to count the roses to realize there

weren't a dozen anymore. Mama happily went back to clucking over her roses like a mother hen. I left the house and delivered the flowers. The surprise and joy on Widow Weiss's face was the same as Mama's when she first had seen the roses. I walked back home. I wondered if Widow Weiss would give one of her roses away to some deserving soul. I had a feeling she would.

# Chapter 19
# The Big Trouble Jar

"װען דער מאָגן איז לײדיק, איז דער קאָפּ אױך לײדיק."
"When the stomach is empty, the head is empty too."

– Mama

Papa left a dollar on the kitchen table every morning for Mama to run the house. In the cellar were burlap sacks of beans, rice, onions, potatoes, flour, and a bushel of apples. Our meals were all planned around the sacks in the cellar and the dollar on the table. If, by some miracle, there was any money left from the dollar at the end of the day, it went into Mama's Big Trouble Jar. She kept it on the highest shelf, way in the back of the kitchen cupboard.

Every once in a while, if one of us kids said we needed money for a pencil or a tablet, Mama would say, "I don't have any more until tomorrow." We would quickly remind her that she had money in the Big Trouble Jar. She would explain that money was not for pencils or notebooks, but only for Big Trouble. Mama used to say, "Do you have to see a cripple or a blind man every day to remind you of the difference between little trouble and big trouble?"

A friend of Papa's talked him into going into business with him. They would need money for the first and last month's rent for a big warehouse, license, gas and electric, plus money to buy rags and metal. When they bought enough to fill a railroad car, and when the price was up, they would sell for a big profit. Papa spread the word among the junk peddlers that they could bring their inventory to the warehouse and get credit and would be paid with a profit when the big check came.

To make a long and miserable story short, Papa's partner watched for the mail, left town with the big check, and Papa was left holding the bag. Money was owed for rent, gas and electric, and the peddlers were owed for their credit and profit.

Papa was in big trouble; Mama and Papa talked clear through the night about what to do now.

The next day Mama took down her Big Trouble Jar. She gave me a nickel and told me to go to the corner grocery store and ask Mr. Right for as many carrots as the nickel would buy. She went to the butcher and bought a big hunk of meat to cut up for *gadempta flaish*. Down she went into the cellar for flour, onions, potatoes, and apples. She baked bread and made *lokshen*. She made a banquet of apple *lokshen, kugel*, and *gadempta flaish* with carrots and potatoes. We dunked the fresh bread in the juice from the meat and had hot tea with apple *lokshen kugel*. It was a wonderful meal and there was enough for seconds, which was very unusual.

Papa enjoyed the meal, but he was appalled that Mama would use the precious Big Trouble Jar for what he called *narishkite* at a time like this. The house rent was due soon. As he complained, Mama said *"zol zine sha,"* and he did.

Papa went back to his horse and wagon. Somehow, he paid his debts as an honest man would, and we survived. The meal became known as the Big Trouble Banquet from the Big Trouble Jar. It is still one of my favorite menus. Mama was right. That meal was food for a Big Troubled Soul.

# Chapter 20
# New Boy in the Neighborhood

"Happiness is like a butterfly;
when it is pursued, it is always beyond your grasp,
but if you sit down quietly, it may light upon you."
– Anonymous

There was a new boy in the neighborhood, and we were thirteen when we met. Irv's family had waited until after his *Bar Mitzvah* to make the move from Youngstown, Ohio to Denver. His father had been the wholesaler for Gelfond's Mayonnaise until Kraft bought them out. They picked Denver because they had an uncle here who thought he could help them start a small business.

Irv was the first perfect gentleman I had ever known. I asked him where he was from, and he asked if he could walk me home. He was so handsome with curly brown hair growing low on his forehead, and a dazzling smile. He was really built well and walked erect with confidence, but not arrogance.

When we walked up the stairs to my porch he lingered and asked if he could kiss me. That had never happened to me before and I said, "No."

"Why don't we count the bricks on the porch by saying 'yes – no – yes – no' and if it comes out 'no' I'll respect that, but if it comes out 'yes' then I get the kiss." It came out NO.

"Look here, there are half bricks at the beginning and the end of the row. That adds up to one brick, so it is really YES." He won and got his kiss. I found out through the years that he always managed to come out the winner.

One early spring evening we were lying on the grass near a lilac bush, watching the fluffy white clouds roll by, picking out imaginary dragons, dogs, fairies and trees. He reached up and plucked a leaf from the fragrant lilac bush. He pinned both of my arms over my head, placed the leaf on my lips and planted a kiss on the leaf. That kiss was an awakening of love for both of us, and we decided to go steady.

I bragged a little about what a great swimmer I was, including the fact that I was a junior lifeguard. "Do you know how to swim?" I asked him.

"No, I don't."

"I will be glad to teach you when summer comes."

"Thanks, that will be great. Where do you swim?"

"We swim at Sloan's Lake."

On the second week in June when the beach opened with a life-guard, we put our clothes on over our swimsuits and headed for the lake. We removed our clothes and placed them in a neat stack on a towel. "Irv, you sit here for a few minutes while I swim out to the raft. When I get back, I'll give you a swimming lesson."

Here was my chance to show off. I waded into the water, turned and waved, dove in, and then, using my most impressive stroke, I swam as fast as I could to the raft. When I reached it, I shook the water from my hair, wiped my eyes and pulled myself up on the raft. To my surprise, Irv sat there beside me grinning, very pleased with himself. I felt like a complete idiot. Imagine the patience, for so many months he kept his secret and let me brag a blue streak.

Although Irv and I were the same age, I was half a year ahead of him in school because his parents moved around a lot. After I graduated from Lake Junior High School and went to West High, he still had half a year in which we could not be together. He just couldn't handle that. He ditched school almost every day and came to West High School to be with me. Mr. Ulamier, the boys' advisor at Lake, called Irv's father to the school, and told him, "I would send him to reform school because of his truancy, but he is such a gentleman I can't make myself do that." All through life Irv got away with murder because he was so polite and charming.

He was finally convinced by his father and the boys' advisor that if he buckled down and passed, he would be going to school with me the next semester, otherwise he would be held back and would be away from me that much longer. He saw the light and graduated with his class. At West when we walked down the hall I would cling to him to the point that my Spanish teacher asked, "Why don't you climb him?"

Every evening after supper Irv would walk up West Colfax to

my house. I watched through the window while he walked and threw little pebbles. About a half a block away he would put two fingers in his mouth and whistle. I then came out on the porch to wait for him. He was always neatly dressed, always wearing a tie. Sport shirts with open collars hit the scene about that time. I think he was the last male in the city of Denver to wear an open collar.

When we were about fourteen, he started to instruct me on how to kiss. "Don't make your lips so hard, make them soft and open your mouth a little."

We were about sixteen when he tried the first French kiss. When he put his tongue into my mouth it was so repulsive. It took a while to get used to it and then I didn't object. One day he told me casually that he loved the style of dresses that buttoned all the way down the front. He didn't fool me. It wasn't the style that interested him. Whenever he could get his hands on his father's car we headed straight for Inspiration Point, overlooking Lakeside Park, where all the young people parked and necked. We would get there at seven in the evening and leave about three in the morning. He was always in trouble with his parents about his late hours. The police would make the rounds and shine a flashlight into the car and tell us it was not safe to be up there so late, and we would straighten our clothes and head home. One night Irv told the policeman that we were married, and the policeman said, "Yah, Yah, and I'm Rin Tin Tin."

Every Saturday night we would get dressed in our best clothes and go dancing. In the winter it was at the Cosmopolitan Hotel and in the summer, it was at Elitch Gardens in the huge Trocadero Ballroom where all the big bands played. We danced to Artie Shaw, Benny Goodman, Les Brown, and many more.

We were now eighteen years old and very much in love. By this time, I knew what love was and could say, "I love you." Five years of heavy necking was starting to take its toll on both of us. He was raised to respect women, and I stayed a virgin, even though I did call him "chicken" once. Irv decided he would quit school and go to work so we could get married, but I would not allow it. I convinced him that if he didn't have a high school diploma he would end up being a janitor. So, we decided that the only answer to our problem was to get married secretly.

He was working in a fruit stand on Saturdays for $1.50 from seven in the morning to seven in the evening. The woman who owned the business didn't trust anyone, probably because so many of her employees had stolen from her. She had a milk bottle in the back room that she used when "nature called."

Everything Irv earned was spent on a good time for us. We rode horseback on Sunday morning, then we each had a hot dog that cost five cents and split a pop to save money. We danced at the wooden dance hall in Morrison, Colorado, until it was washed away during a flood. In the evenings we went to Little Pepino's for spaghetti and beer.

On June 27, 1936, I told my parents I was going to sleep at Eleanor Bernstein's house. Instead, I went to the Argonaut Hotel and checked us in as Mr. and Mrs. Isaacson. I told the desk clerk that Mr. Isaacson would join me at about seven thirty that evening.

"Are you two married?"

"We will be before the night is over." That satisfied him and I was escorted to the room. Irv joined me after work carrying his suit and an orange. I used to get a headache if I didn't eat as soon as I got up in the morning. He had no intention of dashing out of the room the next morning when we awoke. So, the orange was to hold me over until we were ready to leave the room for breakfast.

He showered and changed into his suit, and we left on the bus to the Justice of the Peace in Littleton. There are no horror stories to tell. Mr. Bemis, the Justice of the Peace, was a very nice man. He performed a very respectable ceremony and issued us a beautiful wedding certificate with pink roses on it. He told us he had seen many young people getting married that he worried about, but he was sure that we would do just fine and would be married to each other forever. I don't know if he told everyone that, but we believed him. Irv kissed the bride and put the dime store ring on my finger, and we boarded the bus back to the hotel. When we got to the room and opened the window there was a fountain of water on the roof just outside, and we heard the song, *There's a Small Hotel by a Wishing Well*. Of course, that became our song.

Even after so many years of heavy necking I was still shy and undressed in the bathroom, putting on a very pretty pink satin nighty. I crawled into bed while he changed in the bathroom. He came out in his boxer shorts with three buttons at the waist. He explained that he never slept in pajamas, slipped out of the shorts and got under the covers. I couldn't look. "Does your nighty have fur around the bottom?"

"No, why?"

"The fur could keep your neck warm."

He wanted to leave the lamp on to look at me, but I wasn't comfortable with that. We started the familiar routine of kissing and holding each other close. He slowly tried to get the fur that wasn't there up around my neck. I finally helped him and removed my nighty.

He coaxed me to let him see my body, but I was too shy, and the lamp stayed off. He was a patient and gentle lover. He managed five notches on the bed post that night, and that was the record for our lifetime. The next morning after eating my orange, and more love making, I searched my face in the mirror to see if I looked different. I looked the same, a little tired, but the same. My gallant, satisfied lover told me that never in his wildest dreams did he ever imagine that love could be so wonderfully beautiful.

The next evening, we went to Elitch's to dance. We saw his mother, father, and two brothers there. I was sure they could look at me and know what I had been doing. We walked through the beautiful flower gardens, and the world was ours. We knew without a doubt that no lovers before us ever felt our happiness.

You would think that being married would remove all the guilt, but it didn't. I felt like a slut when we checked into a motel on rare occasions. After we were married a year Irv went shopping with his father and they bought me a beautiful one-carat diamond engagement ring. We had a stupid fight after we were engaged, and I threw the ring at him. So, I broke off our engagement, but we were still married. Of course, we made up and I took the ring back.

Irv wanted to be sure that if I got pregnant at least one person in the world could vouch that we were married. So, he told my brother Isadore, who in turn told my father, so he wouldn't worry about me. My father kept the confidence and never let me know that he knew we were married because he did not want to betray the confidence of my brother.

Finally, when we were twenty years old and each of us was earning $14.00 a week, a grand total of $28.00 a week, we decided it was time to get married "for real." That was July 10, 1938, one day before my birthday. Irv's father sat us down with a pencil and paper and asked us to make a budget. By the time we were through he was on the floor laughing and invited us to move in with them.

I later learned that this was instigated by Irv's very domineering mother who always wanted a daughter but got three sons. She was the kind of woman who wanted me to have everything I wanted, after she had what she wanted. She ran me ragged with her, "Jean, if you want to, would you get me three pounds of onions and ten pounds of potatoes?" I just didn't know how to say, "No." If she asked me to turn off the soup at 1:30, I would call my friend and say I couldn't meet her as we planned because I had to turn off the soup.

My mother-in-law was a poker player but knew her wifely duty was to have a warm meal on the dinner table. Since she played every afternoon and every evening, a good rich soup was the answer. I did learn from her how to make wonderful soups. When I got home from work, even before I could go to the bathroom, she was sitting on the front porch with her coat over her arm waiting for me to take her shopping for the next day's soup.

When she learned that I could sew well she bought up every remnant in town; she had drawers full of material so that I could make her dresses and capes. She always wore capes because she was obese, and they hid her fat. She would take naps in the dresses and wash them in the machine, so they didn't last very long, and the job became endless. Every spare moment I had, after working on a job, was eaten up by her demands for dresses. After a few years I started to balk.

One day Irv's father asked me to go for a walk with him, "Tell me, Jean, why don't you want to sew for Ma?" "She sleeps in the dresses and washes them carelessly."

"Why do you care what she does with them after you make them?"

"Because if she ruins them so quickly then there is never ever an end to the work I have to do, and I am getting tired."

It really didn't change very much after that, but at least my father-in-law understood. While we lived with her, my mother-in-law had a chauffeur in my husband and a maid and dressmaker in me.

Irv learned the "power lesson" from his mother. His father and his older brother had bad tempers and Irv learned that as well. He always told me he loved me and that I was beautiful. I once heard him tell his brother he loved to watch me at the kitchen sink because he loved to look at my behind. I received many, many pats on the fanny during our marriage.

For the first ten years of our marriage, I made it my job never to cause him to lose his temper. I can't remember what he was upset about, but he was ranting and raving about something I did, or didn't do, and I mustered all my courage and said, "Shut up!" He was so shocked he didn't say a word. I found out that I didn't die and he didn't kill me, and I was never afraid of him after that.

*Jean and Irv on their wedding day, July 10, 1938*

# Chapter 21
# Pan

"?ביסטו משוגע"

*"Bist meshuge?"*

"Are you mad?"

– Papa

Pan, a card game that originated in a whorehouse, was a perfect game for such circumstances because the player may leave at any time he is called without disrupting the game.

After the gentleman's mission has been carried out, he simply returns to the table, more relaxed, and resumes playing. Pan is a combination of poker, pinochle, and gin. It is played with ten decks of cards, minus the sevens, eights, and nines. Peculiar expressions, like "muck, pisser, and pecker" are yelled out during the course of the game.

My brother played Pan with five buddies starting right out of high school. My husband was dying to play but the club specified that any newcomer had to watch and learn for two months before he could sit in.

They started to play at 7:30 on Tuesday evening and broke up at 3:30 on Wednesday morning. By the time the fellows were thirty-five they talked it over and decided that 2:30 was late enough. When they reached forty-five, they started to run through the deck until 1:30. At fifty-five it seemed sensible to quit at 12:30. It was a shock to all of them when they hit the big six-O. "It was-all right, already, at 11:30."

Irv loved to gamble. Pan had become a passion, and he enjoyed the camaraderie with the guys.

Let's get back to the days when the young studs were playing until 3:30. He literally lived from Tuesday to Tuesday, and I swear if our daughter got married or had a baby on Tuesday, you could count him out. I often told him that I wished there was something in the world that could excite me that way. But then he enjoyed every-thing he did to the nth degree, so how could I expect Pan to be any different?

It became my unpleasant task to get Irv out of bed for work after two hours of sleep. After a quick shower, a gulp of coffee and a peck on the cheek, he would *shlep* out to the car, bleary eyed. He coasted through his workday half asleep, staggered home, flopped on the couch and was asleep before I could say, "Disgusting." He awoke a few hours later, ate a light supper and at once went to sleep for the night.

Every Wednesday morning, we went through the same ritual. It was next to impossible to get him up for work. On my first try, I gently touched his shoulder, and pleasantly whispered, "Honey, it's time to get up." Five minutes later came the second attempt, a little louder with a trace of irritation in my voice. I shook him this time, "Honey, if you don't get up now you won't have time to eat breakfast." I hung in there, now my third effort, still louder with my exasperation clearly evident, "Come on, get your butt out of bed or you will be late for work." Finally, there was no more time to waste so, at the top of my voice, "I am getting sick and tired of this Wednesday morning business. Believe me, next week you will set your own alarm and if you don't get up, then tough, you don't get up. I don't give a darn. I am not your mother!"

By this time Irv is almost awake and is completely oblivious of my valiant struggle to arouse him. All he knows for sure is that the sweet thing he made love to yesterday has turned into a screaming mimi. "Why do you have to be so rough when you wake me? Why can't you wake me with a nice kiss, like I do you?"

Undaunted, this warrior entered the battle ground again. The next Wednesday I tried his suggested system. I leaned over and kissed my darling gently on the lips. I have no idea what dream stage he was in, but I scared him half to death. He jumped up swinging his fists at some horrendous attacker. It was all I could do to jump out of the way to avoid a broken jaw. He barked, "What the hell is the matter with you, scaring me like that?"

Marriage, I give up. Whichever course you pursue, it's the wrong one.

The following week, I was still wide awake when he sauntered in at a quarter to four in the morning. I sat upright in bed, placed my fists on my hips and announced, "I am going to put a stop to this."

He smiled and asked, "How?"

# Chapter 22
# The Target

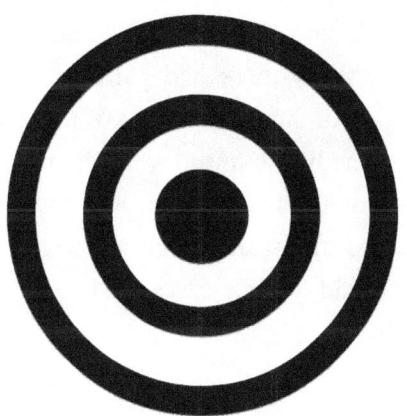

"...לאַכן מיט ווייטיק; שמייכלען מיט טרערן אין האַרצן."

"...Lachen mit veytik."

"...Laughing with pain; smiling with tears in one's heart."

– Mama

My high school English teacher told me to look up jenny in the dictionary – it meant a female jackass.

When I graduated from high school, I began to use the name Jean whenever I filled out a job application. I was soon known as Jean. Mama was insulted because I had changed my name.

After I was married and had a baby, I felt like a prisoner. I was stuck in the house. If I didn't get out, I would lose my mind. I joined a group that met every Tuesday night to raise funds to educate the orphans of the Holocaust. I sneezed or coughed at the wrong moment because all of a sudden, I was president and in charge of all committees and the yearly fund raiser.

Forty hands went up when I asked for help. There were now two weeks left to count down and seven loyal helpers were still working with me. The other thirty-three had gallbladder or bladder operations, grandmother died, family went out of town, etc.

I couldn't leave the house until Irv got home because he was the "babysitter." This was the fourth night in a row I was waiting with my coat on, puckered up for the quick goodbye kiss. As he walked through the door I said, "Honey, your dinner is on the stove. Put Candy to bed at seven."

"Just a minute."

"Honey, I'll be late."

""Jean – just a minute. You come back or I won't be here when you get home."

So, I came back.

"Sit down."

I sat down, fidgeting. My husband took a piece of paper and drew a target. "What is the most important thing in your life?"

"You, dear."

"No, you are the most important thing in your life. Put your name in the bullseye. If the baby is sick, then, of course, you move out of the bullseye until she is well. What is the next most important?"

"You, dear."

"Okay, put me on the first line. Next?"

We continued as I fidgeted…family, friends, home, hobbies, etc.

"Where is this club that has taken over your life?"

"It's not even on the target…"

When we finished, he said, "Okay, now I know you're committed. We will talk about this later. Go on, get out of here."

Whenever life becomes too much to handle, I draw a target. I put myself in the bullseye and in a minute, I can see what is important.

# Chapter 23
# The Big Crush

"The greatest sin of maturity is losing one's zest for life."
– Anonymous

I t was January 1942. Irv and I were twenty-four years old, and the shock of Pearl Harbor was setting in. The draft was in full swing, and we were worried about that. There were three boys in the Isaacson family, and two boys in the Slosky family who were next door neighbors and friends. In the summer I would sit with the five guys on the front porch, eating watermelon, spitting the seeds as far as we could, and singing at the top of our voices. It was a wonderful time that the war was about to change.

Irv's oldest brother Paul was a doctor, and he was not drafted. Irv was married and had a baby, so he was not drafted yet, but the middle boy, Ted, was taken into the army. Herman Slosky was in medical school, so he was not drafted. Robert, the younger one, was about to be drafted so he enlisted in the Air Corps. We were sad to see him go off to Officers Training School. He came home in his gorgeous officer's uniform, for his farewell visit before being shipped overseas for active duty. He looked so glamorous and handsome to me.

While he was flying combat missions from England over Germany, I wrote letters and sent chocolate chip cookies to him. I was now admitting to myself that I had a crush on him. Now the tone of my letters was changing, and the cookies were being sent more often. When he wrote to us, he never mentioned the letters or cookies, because he wasn't sure that Irv knew about that. That added to the intrigue, and I read many things between the lines that may not have been there. It was all very confusing to me because it did not change my feelings for my husband – I loved him. Was it possible to love two men at the same time?

Now his letters were signed "Bob" instead of Robert. After fifty missions he was sent home for R&R. I can't recall how it came about, whether Irv invited Bob or I did, but he slept in our spare bedroom for three days and nights. He got up only to go to the bathroom, get a drink of water, or eat a light meal. Irv went off to work every day and I was home alone with Bob. On the fourth day Bob seemed to be over his stupor and we sat and talked.

"How do you people live like this? You get up at the same time every day, you eat the same breakfast, go off to the same job at the same time, eat lunch in the same restaurant, come home to the same house and the same people, and then do the same thing day after day. I would go crazy."

Wow, he sounded so exciting and worldly to me and he made my life seem so dull. I felt like a boring person who had never been past the corner drugstore. That just couldn't be right because I was happy every day and awoke glowing to be alive, young, and loved. I looked forward to Irv coming home every evening with his big smile, giving me a kiss and a hug, and a pat on the fanny when I washed the dishes. He whispered lewd little hints about what would be in store for me that night. I was confused.

I was wearing a pair of harem pants made of silk jersey that clung to every crease and crevice. I pretended not to be aware of the effect they had on Bob. He asked, "How come you wear such tight pants?"

"Oh, they weren't always this tight, I have gained some weight," I lied.

"How would you like to go down to the Cosmopolitan Hotel to the Officers' Club and have a drink with me?"

"I would love to."

It was a beautiful winter day, and the snow was gently falling. I wore a pink lacy wool scarf and felt pretty because pink was my best color. Besides, I had once read that if you wore pink the first time a man met you, he would never forget you.

Bob indicated to the hostess that he wanted the booth in the far corner of the room. It was darker there. He put our wraps on the upholstered bench on one side of the booth, and I slid in on the other side. He slid in beside me and we ordered our drinks. I had forgotten to wear gloves, and my hands were cold, so I wrapped them around the brandy snifter that held a lit candle.

"Are your hands cold? Here, let me warm them."

He took my hands and started to rub them. Then he lifted them close to his mouth and blew hot breath to warm them. He inched closer and I could feel his thigh against mine, but I didn't move away. I still had not had my first drink, but my stomach was getting warm.

"How many English girls did you go out with?"

"A few."

"Any one special?"

"They were all nice."

"Were you frightened when you flew your bombing missions? I would think you would be petrified."

"Of course, I was scared. After each flight, the law of averages increased against me. I watched my buddies' planes being shot down. When we returned to our base, we waited breathlessly to see how many of the group returned or didn't come back."

I told him that I used to watch the news, and when the casualties were given my heart was in my mouth. I once heard an announcer say the average life span of a bomber pilot was eighteen minutes in the air, but I am sure that was an exaggeration.

We were on our second drink when he took my chin in his hand and turned my head to face him. He looked into my eyes and asked, "What would you do if I asked you to go upstairs to a room with me?"

I was naive and protected at the time, and answered exactly what I felt, "I would probably cry and run home."

I am sure he was thoroughly disgusted with this tease. I blew out the candle in the snifter and the booth lost its luster. He didn't press the issue and soon we were on our way home. What he doesn't know to this day is that the crush was over, because I couldn't believe that he would betray his friend. I admitted to myself that I was equally to blame.

When we got home, I turned on the lamp by the easy chair and handed Bob the paper to read while I fixed dinner. At dinner, Bob and I didn't look at each other. Irv did all the talking and we both spoke only to Irv. I would like to see the day you could fool Irv. He watched us with what he used to laughingly call his "side eye." You could have cut the air with a knife, and I didn't like it. Looking forward to an entire evening of this was more than I could stand, so I suggested, "Why don't you guys go to the basketball game? We are in second place. If we win tonight, we'll be in first place. It should be exciting."

"That sounds great, what do you think, Bob?"

"Fine. I'd like that."

"Jean, would you like to go with us?"

"No thanks, I am working on a project, and this will be a great time for me to finish it."

I was reading in bed when I heard the garage door at eleven thirty. I quickly turned out the lamp and pretended I was asleep. I wasn't in the mood for the third degree I knew was coming.

The next morning at breakfast Bob said, "Well, I guess I have imposed on you nice people long enough. I'll move on home today. Thanks for everything."

Years later Irv accused me of having an affair with Bob. My answer to him was, "Whenever a man cheats on his wife, he accuses her of having an affair." I never heard another word about that again, but I know it was on his mind.

Irv has been dead for over two years now. Can you believe that at age seventy-four, all the old fantasies and feelings are in full swing. I guess I am trying to replace Irv. Bob has been a commanding officer at an air base in California all these years. His brother Herman told me that Bob's wife is terribly ill with the worst kind of emphysema. Everything comes full circle – I have the urge to write to him and tell him how sorry I am that his wife is ill.

# Chapter 24
# The War

"אויב איינער וואַרפט שטיינער אויף דיר, וואַרפט צוריק ברויט."

*"Aoyb eyner varft shteyner aoyf dir, varft tsurik broyt."*

"If someone casts stones at you, throw back bread."

— Papa

When World War II started, Irv became a civilian employee at Lowry Field. He taught personnel work to officers and the G.I.s. The draft board was apparently satisfied with his status, and he was not drafted until they got to the married men with children. By this time our daughter, Candy, was already two years old. He was inducted at Fort Logan, and we felt very lucky because his basic training would be so close to home. He would have six weeks of basic training and then go overseas.

It sounds impossible, but on his very first night in the army he was put on guard duty from seven in the evening to seven the next morning. They shoved a rifle in his hand, told him to walk back and forth in front of the gate with the rifle on his shoulder. "If someone approaches, hold the rifle in both hands and say, 'Halt and be recognized.'"

Simple enough. Any moron could do that. At seven forty-five someone approached the gate. Irv stood at attention with his rifle in his hands and said, "Halt and be recognized!"

The approaching officer stopped and said, "Colonel Jack Conner approaching."

They stared at each other for a minute and then my brilliant husband said, "So...I recognize you, what the hell do I do now?"

He was very lucky the Colonel had a sense of humor. He questioned Irv and found out it was his very first day in the army. He patiently explained the proper procedure, saluted Irv, and told him to return the salute. It turned out that Colonel Conner was Irv's C.O. They became good friends, as close as an officer and a G.I. could get.

I had never driven a car before, but I would be damned if Irv was going to be so close to me and I would not see him. I got into the old Chevy with Candy and stood her behind me. I turned the key in the ignition. You have never ever heard such an awful sound. I quickly turned the key off and then tried again. This time the motor turned over and I was in business. I stripped the gears, stepped on the gas and the car jerked forward for a full half block. When we got to the corner, I stepped on the brake. My daughter and I almost went through the windshield. After several ghastly starts I reached Sheridan Boulevard, and I was heading south. With never a thought that I didn't have a driver's license, I rode merrily on my way. Someone had told me to look for an old water tower and that would be Fort Logan.

The guard stopped me and asked me a few questions for which I had no answers. He then let me explain why I was there and suggested that I drive to the parade grounds where the new G.I.s were drilling. I jerked the car away from the gate and finally saw three groups of soldiers. A Sergeant was barking orders, and I laughingly watched the comedy of the boys turning every direction, bumping into each other, and frustrating the Sergeant. I was laughing but the Drill Sergeant was not. I got out of the car and stood against a tree trying to find my husband. My Candy yelled, "Daddy!" and three hundred heads turned in her direction. It was a very sad and emotional moment.

The Sergeant barked, "Lunch! Chow time, half an hour! Fall out!"

Irv had spotted us and came running. He explained he had only a half hour to eat so we could not visit. He was very upset about my taking Candy in the car without a license or any knowledge of driving. Well – there was nothing he could do about it. He walked away from us backwards and bumped into a pole, spun around and jogged to the dining hall.

We talked on the phone every night and he said he would be able to get an overnight pass on the third weekend. Happy day! Six weeks later he shipped overseas to what we later learned was England. All of these new recruits, married men with children, were in the invasion of Normandy. Many were slaughtered. Irv was hit with shrapnel in the back and leg. He was sent back to an English hospital and was back on duty in France in four weeks.

My husband was with the first group of G.I.s to enter the Auschwitz concentration camp. I recall many years later when people were trying to deny the Holocaust ever existed. I could see him clenching his teeth and turning red, but he didn't talk about it.

The Army realized that many of the Jewish soldiers could speak *Yiddish* and so could be understood by the survivors. There were eleven Jewish soldiers that became interpreters and record keepers. They provided comfort to those who were in a state of grief and misery. Irv got up on an old table and they gathered around to hear what he had to say. They all looked so frightened. They didn't know how it could be worse, but they knew the soldiers were enemies of Germany, and they were German.

He said, "Do not be afraid. We are enemies of Germany, but we are not your enemies. We are here to help you. As you see the gates are open. You are free to go but I see none of you are trying to leave. Of course, where would you go? We will feed and clothe you and try to help with your medical problems. We will gather information from you that may help you find your families. If you have family in America, give us this information also and we will contact them for you.

"You are free – free to do anything you wish. We will try to help you in any way possible. G-d bless all of you." By this time Irv's eyes were full and he couldn't see anything.

The very first man Irv interviewed was twenty-six years old, but he looked seventy. He looked like he was ready to pass out, so Irv quickly gave him a candy bar, which he swallowed practically whole. He then fell to the floor, vomited, and died. I could never get my husband to talk much about his experiences, but after that sight and smell he was the "last angry man"! It really left its mark on his personality. He was very conscious and very aware of anything that smacked of anti-Semitism and probably overreacted on many occasions because of this experience.

# Chapter 25
# The War is Over

**THE DENVER POST**

| VOL. 8 | COMPLETE NEWS COVERAGE | 10 10 |
|---|---|---|
| VOL. 45 | DENVER, COLORADO, MONDAY, MAY 1, 1945 | EXTRA |

# THE WAR IS OVER!

## GERMANY SURRENDERS

### UNCONDITIONAL ACCEPTANCE OF ALLIED TERMS SIGNED AT 2:41 A. M.

## PRESIDENT PROCLAIMS VICTORY IN EUROPE

"The Ten Commandments are non-negotiable."
– Anonymous

The Germans surrendered May 7, 1945. Thank G-d the war is over, and Irv is coming home. My last letter from him told me that he was one of the GIs that entered a concentration camp. "It's too horrible to write about. I will tell you everything someday when I can talk about it. I was just advised that I will be home on the 29th of May. Warm up the bed."

I can't believe this day has finally come. Irv's plane will land in Denver at 1 AM. He will be home for lunch. I am lying in bed wide awake at four in the morning. It is still pitch dark and I am looking out of the window staring at the sky full of twinkling stars. It is almost a full moon, but I can't see it. I am talking to the absent sun, coaxing it to hurry up and rise. Did I forget anything? I really tried my best to make everything perfect for him.

I reached over to his side of the bed knowing it would be empty, but not for long. I pulled his pillow to me and hugged it as I had done for four hundred and seven nights. How I dreamed and fantasized about this wonderful day until nothing else existed. Candy was two years old! Eight more hours! I closed my eyes and finally fell asleep.

Irv is slowly inching his way off the plane and it's 11:15 AM. He'll really be home for lunch. I told him not to eat the junk on the plane because I had his favorite lunch waiting. For eleven long months he had dreamed of this moment. Damn it! There are fifty other GIs waiting for every taxi. Irv sprints up the ramp about a block long, hoping to grab a cab before it got in the designated pick-up lane. After the longest forty-five minutes of his life a cab finally stopped for him. He was clutching a precious box with cashmere sweaters for me and the baby. In his pocket are two gold bracelets: a real beauty for each of us.

He knew I always loved it when he brought me one rose, so he asked the cabby to stop at a florist. Rose in hand, they were crossing the West Colfax viaduct when he saw the icehouse and Star Bakery. As they crossed Federal Boulevard, he saw all the old familiar stores he used to frequent: Cohen's Bakery with a window full of bagels, Fried's Drug Store where the kids hung out, and Segal's Gas station where he had worked part time. Old people he recognized walked a little more stooped than when he last saw them. It felt warm.

I called the airport. His plane had landed on time...he should be here by now! I hope I look OK. I never know when to quit. I've been trying to do too much. I didn't want to look tired when he got here. Oh well, it's too late now. The baby just had a bath and is wearing a new little outfit I made. My hair was freshly washed, and I was wearing short shorts with a bare tank top. That should do it.

Irv hadn't slept the night before. He boozed it up pretty good with the guys. He was really bushed, but don't worry, he'd stay awake tonight, you can bet on that. The cab pulled up in front of the house and Irv paid him. "Man, the house looks great. All the wood trim is freshly painted white. She didn't have money for that, so she had to do it herself. The lawn is all edged. We don't have an electric edger so she must have plenty of blisters to show for it. Bless her heart, she always had to do everything herself. Well, I'm here to help her now!"

The yard looked beautiful. Red geraniums lined the walk and encircled the trees. Two hanging plants hung from the porch, filled with cascading petunias in shades of purple, lavender, pink, and white with green tendrils falling. "She ate plenty of leftovers to be able to buy those flowers," he thought.

Oh G-d, I hear the key in the lock. I can hardly breathe. I grab Candy and run to greet him. We practically squashed the baby between us, hugging and kissing. It was wonderful feeling the warmth seeping through us. The "I Love Yous" and the "I've Missed Yous" were repeated over and over. We hugged and kissed and cried and could not let go of each other. He used to love to grab my hips and pull me to him, but the baby was in the way. He took a deep breath and sat down in the favorite chair he had dreamed about almost as much as he dreamed about me.

I put Candy in his arms. He was self-conscious and apprehensive. She was warm and smelled so good. He quipped, "She has my features and your fixtures. Oops, she's wet!" He held her out, stiff-armed. We both laughed. I told Irv I would fix his lunch just as soon as I changed Candy and fed her. Then I would put her down for her nap.

When I came back, he grabbed my wrists and pulled me down on the rug in front of his chair. I put my arms around his waist and laid my head in his lap. He stroked my hair and then cupped my face in his hands and kissed my closed eyes. He then asked to see my hands. My nails were filed down short because I had broken most of them by scraping paint and gardening. He turned my hands over and looked at my palms and he said, "Oh, I knew it. Look at those blisters." And he kissed the sores. "From now on that's my job," he whispered.

I got up to fix lunch and the phone rang. It was my girlfriend, the one who, if you told her the house was on fire, would still have one more thing to tell you. I finally got rid of her and no sooner did I hang up when the phone rang. Again. It was my mother wanting to talk to her favorite son-in-law. Irv pantomimed that he was in the shower and would call her back. I finally got rid of her. While I was fixing lunch, Irv called to tell me the dog was sick and retching. By the time I got there the dog had vomited on the rug. Irv just sat there, like a stranger. I ran to get soap and water to clean the rug and the dog. Oh, it smelled awful. Oh heck! I wanted everything to be so perfect. It wasn't the way I planned at all. With the dog in the yard and my hands washed, I finished lunch. He relished every bite of the lamb on his favorite light Jewish rye, iced tea with mint from the garden, and apple pie ala mode. He was satisfied and left a tip. He always did that when he liked the meal.

I started to clean up the kitchen. Irv said, rather sharply, that he was going to lie down for a minute. As he walked into the bedroom, I heard him mumble something under his breath that sounded very much like the sh— word I hated. I dropped everything, dried my hands, and walked into the bedroom where he was stretched out on the bed. I untied his heavy G.I. shoes and pulled them off. I pulled the damp socks away from the soles of his feet. He smiled and outstretched his arms, inviting me to join him on the bed. We wrapped our arms around each other and did some serious wet kissing. He unbuttoned the front of my tank top. I followed his cue and unbuttoned his shirt. He kissed my closed eyelids. I heard the baby whimper and then she really started crying. I slid off the bed and as I walked out, I again heard the sh— word under his breath.

I walked back in, cradling the whimpering baby and told Irv that she was as hot as fire, and that I thought I had better call the doctor. I came back and told him that the doctor wanted me to bring her into his office at once. "Do you want to come with me?"

He said, "No, I am bushed and will take a little nap until you get back." It turned out Candy had an ear infection, and I had to stop at the store for a prescription. The poor little thing was so cranky. Irv was really sawing wood when I got home. I sponged the baby to get her fever down, gave her liquid aspirin and put her down. She was asleep in no time. I thought about his tone when he said he would stay home. He had sounded very irritated. Why was he mad at me? I couldn't help it. It wasn't anything I had planned. Damn!

I went back into the kitchen to finish the clean-up job. I was facing the sink refilling the pickle jar when Irv startled me as he playfully grabbed me from behind. I dropped the pickle jar on the floor. The glass broke and pickles and brine were everywhere. Irv just stood there in shock. I yelled. "Well, don't just stand there like a glump! Take out the trash!"

He yelled back, "I won't pop to! I had enough of taking orders in the army. I thought I was through with that when I came home. Son of a bitch! What happened to you while I was gone? You never used to order me around. What happened to, 'Please, dear, will you take out the trash?'" I started to cry. What was happening to us? I sounded just like Virginia Woolf.

"Oh, sh——. I can't stand it when you cry. I'm a selfish bastard. It isn't your fault. What's the matter with me, like I don't know?"

Between awful sobs, I blurted out, "Well, I'm not the only one who has changed. You were always helpful, and you never used that awful language. That might go with your army buddies, but I am not comfortable with it. Also, you were never sharp with me. We could always talk things out."

Irv was ashamed of himself, and he got stubborn and stamped out of the kitchen and went back into the bedroom. He undressed and put on his new tee shirt and PJ bottoms and got under the covers. On second thought he hopefully slipped out of the bottoms and put them on the bedside chair.

When I came back into the bedroom to apologize for my behavior, he was fast asleep. I undressed and slid into the bed very quietly. There was no question, he was very tired. I got out of bed at six thirty the next morning when I heard the baby. I dressed us both, got the dog, and went next door to Millie, my good friend and neighbor. I knew she got up early too. I told her my sad tale of woe, and she suggested that I leave the dog and the baby with her until after the baby's afternoon nap. That's just what I had hoped for.

When Irv awoke, he reached across to my side of the bed. I wasn't there. He opened his eyes, and the sun was streaming in the window. "Oh G-d, I slept through the night." He jumped out of bed and slipped into his PJ bottoms and walked through the house calling my name. I was nowhere to be found, and the baby and the dog were gone. "I'll bet she is mad at me. I don't blame her. I'm mad at myself too. Sh——, this is my first day back and she can't stay home." He took a shower and shaved and walked out of the bathroom with the proverbial towel around his waist. I was standing there in tiny lace panties and a bra with a Mona Lisa smile.

"I took the baby and the dog to Millie, next door. She is going to keep them until after Candy's afternoon nap. We have about eight hours to ourselves. I promised to do the same for her when Bill comes home. What would you like for breakfast?"

"Breakfast, are you crazy?" He took me in his arms and then suddenly let go. "What's wrong?"

"Just a minute. I forgot something. I've got to take the receiver off the hook."

It's good to have money and the things money can buy, but it's good, too, to check up once in a while and make sure you haven't lost the things that money can't buy.

# Chapter 26
# The Veteran

"…(you) shall not pervert judgement…"
– Deuteronomy 16:19

The law stated that veterans were entitled to return to the job that they had to leave when they were drafted. That was easier said than done. Irv's job at Lowry no longer existed. It was his responsibility to find a job for which he was qualified in any Federal agency. He could bump an employee if he outranked the person in the position by the years of his military service added to his civil service. However, he couldn't bump a veteran regardless of the circumstances. Of course, he didn't get cooperation or information, nor could he make friends when they recognized that he might be able to take their jobs. He finally figured out that the Civil Service Commission had the information he needed, and he found a personnel job, Grade 12, held by a woman who had much less time than he did, and was not a veteran. He went out to the Rocky Mountain Arsenal and started steps to bump Helen Barton out of her job. She laughed at him and said the commanding officer was a dear friend of hers and he would protect her job.

Irv came home that evening and told me he would bet that Helen was sleeping with the Colonel. It turned out that he was right. He did get her job, she was reduced to Grade 11, and she never forgot it. Ms. Barton could not handle being the loser and having Irv as her boss. She started to drink and got into a very bad accident driving home from work drunk. When Irv told me about it, he did not smile, but I could read something in his eyes, and I said, "He who enjoys the catastrophes of others will not go unpunished." He assured me that as much as he disliked Helen, he would never wish anything like that on anyone, and we dropped the subject.

By the time a year was up Irv had made many friends, and everyone trusted him because he turned heaven and earth to promote anyone who had been demoted. His sense of fairness was one of the things I loved about him. Irv was in the supermarket one day when he bumped into an old army buddy. He was shuffling along with two canes and was in obvious pain. "Tony, let's go have a beer and talk, what do you say?" Both men finished their shopping. Irv called to say he would be late but to hold his dinner.

It turned out that Tony Amato had been in a fox hole for two weeks in cold, damp mud up to his thighs. He later developed M.S. but with hard work and relentless therapy Tony was able to get around with the two canes. He told Irv he was having no luck getting a job because of the disability. "Tony, come out to the Rocky Mountain Arsenal tomorrow morning, and I'll find some job you can do. I know you were a bookkeeper; you don't need legs for that." He was legally and certainly morally entitled to bump into a job that was held by a non-vet.

He bumped into the cashier's job. Nobody was fired, employees just went down one grade. Of course, you always make someone unhappy when you bump, and the wheels started to turn to try to get Tony to quit. His office was moved from the main floor to the second floor. This meant that he had to punch in on the second floor, go downstairs, pick up the heavy bag of coins and bills and go upstairs to the office, struggling with two canes. Pretty cruel, I would say.

Irv couldn't bear to watch Tony struggle, so he offered to get the cash bag, bring it up to him, and return it in the evening. The safe wasn't open before or after regular working hours so there was no way Irv could do it except by taking time from his own job. He told the timekeeper to charge him for ten minutes every evening and every morning. Over a period of two years, it used up some of Irv's vacation time, but that was OK. Then they started to complain about Irv since he didn't have the authority to handle the cash bags. Tony signed a statement, as did Irv, that they would be responsible for any money that was missing, which, of course, there never was.

My husband used to meet Tony at the building entrance every morning and evening and park his car, then bring it back when it was time to go home. He finally had it "up to here" and he marched into the adjutant's office and endeared himself with this sermon.

"Major, how in the hell can you look yourself in the mirror when you shave? How much trouble would it be to give Tony one of the empty rooms on the main floor to end his misery? Shame on you."

I honestly don't know how I rated this wonderful man. I remember Irv saying, in a bragging manner, "You can judge a man by the woman that will have him." I was sure it was a compliment.

When Tony died the entire executive staff came to the funeral. Tony's teenage kids asked Irv to be a pallbearer. He later sat with me and said, "I am having trouble trying not to vomit when I look at all those hypocritical, cruel bastards. It wouldn't have cost them one cent to be kind to Tony when he was alive. They will probably go back and have coffee and donuts in his memory. Sh—."

In every department on a military installation there is a civilian and a military person on the same level. The military are transferred around a great deal and are not on one job long. Irv had a new adjutant about every six months. They ranged from twenty-two-year-old kids, as he referred to them, to old, stuffy officers who were carried away with their importance. Irv put a framed motto on his wall. It read, "Thou shalt not take thyself too seriously." I don't think it helped. One day the new adjutant, Major Butler, came up to see Irv and told him he had a buddy that had just retired from the army and was looking for a job. The Major knew they had an opening for which they were interviewing at the time. It was Irv's job to pick the top qualified three and select from them. He gave the Major an application for his friend and told him to call for an appointment.

When the gentleman, and I use the word loosely, walked in he was "drunk as a skunk." He hit every piece of furniture he passed, he was bleary-eyed, and his speech was slurred. Irv told me that night that the guy smelled so bad from secondhand whiskey that he had to move his chair a couple of feet away to survive. He talked to the applicant for five minutes, which was five minutes more than he needed, and told him he would be advised by mail if selected. Then Irv walked into Major Butler's office.

"Major, I am sorry, there isn't a chance in hell that your buddy can be hired. It is illegal, he was out qualified, outranked, and is not eligible. Besides, he has never worked for the government, he has none of the abilities I need, and he came in so drunk I couldn't even find out if maybe I could find something else for him. You will be gone in six months, and I will be stuck with a drunk that can't perform under any circumstances. I am really sorry. I would like to do you the favor, but this is way out of line."

The Major got very angry, red as a beet, pointed his finger and touching Irv's nose, as he yelled, "This isn't over, Isaacson. You will get your wings clipped and your legs chopped before I am through with you. I will not forget this, and I will fix it so all other military men coming in here will be briefed about you, and not in a good way, you can be damned sure of that."

"Would you care to put that in writing, sir?"

He meant what he said. He started a whispering campaign against Isaacson. He spread the word at every drinking party, every meeting, and never missed a chance to tell anyone who would listen what a bastard Irv was. A new young lieutenant came in under Major Butler, and, in order to get on his good side, told him, "I know how to get rid of Isaacson, leave it to me."

Lieutenant Brooks called Irv in one day, motioned to him to sit down and lit his pipe with much ado, letting Irv "sweat." "Isaacson, have you ever thought about retiring?"

"Why do you ask?"

"Well, I heard it is not very pleasant around here for you and from what I hear it is going to get worse."

"Are you threatening me, Lieutenant?"

"Oh, I wouldn't go that far."

"Who did you promise you would get rid of me?"

"Why...no one. That's a ridiculous thing to say."

"Oh, it is, is it? Well let me tell you something, squirt. You are not my superior. You're young enough to be my son. Thank G-d you are not. I would really be ashamed of you if you were."

"Believe me, Isaacson, you would be smart to think about what I said because it is not going to get better. It is going to get worse. You are dismissed."

"Are you threatening me?"

"I said you are dismissed, Isaacson."

"Lieutenant, sir, I would appreciate your kind offer in writing, and I will reply in the same manner."

Operation "Destroy Isaacson" started. Helen Barton was the first one to get on the bandwagon. A reorganization chart was drawn up to demote Irv and put Helen back in the boss's chair. A new job description for a position was written up with every ridiculous qualification that no one on earth could meet but Major Butler's buddy – two years of gunnery school, four years in the engineering corps, and M.P. duty. None of these things were in any way related to the work in the office. Irv was demoted from Grade 12 to Grade 11, and Helen was now a Grade 12, and the drunk's desk was placed next to Irv's. The demotion did not change Irv's paycheck because there is a regulation that says that his pay would continue for two years to provide an adjustment period. This applies if you are demoted through a reorganization and by no fault of your own.

A year later another reorganization took place. This time Irv was demoted to Grade 7. It was illegal because he should have been allowed to bump, but they ignored the regulation. With each illegal change Irv put in an appeal. The appeals were placed in a drawer and were never processed until Irv brought them the regulation that set the time limit for a reply. They then sent the appeal to headquarters in Washington where they had twelve months to answer. The military buddy system was in full swing. Calls were made to the Pentagon explaining that "this guy is a bastard so handle it accordingly." One day the adjutant told Irv he had too much principle. When he came home and told me about this bright remark, I told him that he had better not compromise his principles because that was what I loved most about him. He liked that. Irv explained to me that he was being very quiet while they produced a pattern of illegal activities. "I am going to hire a civil service lawyer now. I don't care what it costs me. I am going to fight this fight for me and all the poor *shnooks* who are afraid they will lose their jobs. Everybody lets them get away with the garbage because they are scared. They have families and what they have is better than nothing."

When the first legal letter hit the Arsenal, addressed to "Eyes Only" Commanding Officer, you know what hit the fan. The General didn't like this kind of attention, and he wanted action. They were running around trying to find a way to show that action was being taken. That was hard to do, and they were all pretty upset.

One of the supervisors from another building was standing near Irv's desk, looking out the window. Karl Schmidt said to him, "Too bad, Hitler should have finished the job. Too bad." Irv didn't say a word, but he was boiling.

As he later walked through the parking lot to get his car, he took his ignition key and scratched Karl's new red Thunderbird from front to back. He never heard a word about it. I told him I didn't think that was very nice and he said, "Well, Darling, Karl Schmidt isn't very nice either, so we are even."

Irv had satisfaction when Major Butler's drunken buddy did not pass his probationary period. He was late too often, absent too often, and drunk too often.

Helen Barton was now in control. Irv was demoted again to Grade 5 and transferred to a desk in a warehouse. All the time Irv was handing his certificates of outstanding performance to his lawyer. He also had suggestions that were accepted that were of benefit to the government, and letters of commendation from Lowry and Fitzsimons for help he gave to the personnel office. No one could ever dare say he was not doing a good job.

In February 1965 we had the coldest six weeks in the history of Colorado. The warehouse where Irv's desk was had four canvas flaps, one on each side of the square building. These were raised when a truck drove through. Irv left for work looking like he lived at the North Pole. Two pairs of woolen socks, rubber boots over his shoes, tee shirts under a flannel wool shirt, a sweater over that, gloves with fur lining, and an army surplus fur-lined jacket with a fur-lined hood. I asked him if the heater was broken in his car. "Why do you have to dress like that to work in an office?" He then told me where he worked. I started to cry and begged him to quit. We would find a way to survive. I knew he wouldn't quit. He was like a bulldog.

"Jean, you know the restroom I am supposed to use is an outhouse, a two-seater one. I get into my car and drive down to the next building and use their restrooms. Today the supervisor in the building told me I was wasting too much time. Instead, I was to use the restroom nearest to my desk. I told him, 'Listen, Giles, when I see you and your bare ass, two sheets to the wind in that cold outhouse, then I will join you.'"

Irv saved every ridiculous memo, every personnel action, every letter, and many other documents he should never have seen. There were now two factions at the Arsenal, "For Isaacson" and "Against Isaacson." The "For" group mailed him everything that there was the least chance that he could use. Nobody dared to talk to Irv. They would lower their eyes in the cafeteria or look the other way. They were afraid and he understood. The two men that remained friends with Irv were harassed so badly they finally transferred to another agency.

After ten years of appeals and two hearings with an arbitrator his case was finally scheduled for Federal Court. Before it was over Irv would pay his lawyer fourteen thousand dollars.

Court was scheduled to start at 8:30 AM but Bob Coopersmith, his lawyer, was told to be in the judge's chambers at 8:00 AM. We waited in the hall for him. He came out of the judge's chambers as white as a sheet. You couldn't tell where his lips began or ended. He had gotten out of a sick bed after a heart attack to be there.

He took us into a small room for the attorney's use, no window, just a table and four chairs. We sat down. "Well, Irv, we hit the jackpot. A Jewish lawyer and a Jewish client, and an Arab judge. The good news is I have had cases before Judge Habib before and have always found him to be fair and honest. The bad news is, he will give me ten minutes to convince him this is not a frivolous case. Ten minutes! I can't even present my introductory statement in ten minutes."

Irv was very worried about Bob. "Listen, Bob. Nobody is going to get sick or die over this case. You have done everything humanly possible to prepare for this day. If it goes wrong, it is not your fault. Nobody will blame you. We are in this together. We know you did the very best you could and that's good enough for Jean and me."

"OK, let's go on in." In the hall Bob said, "Judge Habib has a pet peeve, or an idiosyncrasy, call it what you will; he can't stand it when a briefcase is on the table. So, when we sit down, take everything you need out of your briefcase, put it neatly on the table and put the briefcase on the shelf under your chair."

"Hear ye, hear ye, this court is now in session. Honorable Judge Habib presiding. Please rise." The Judge came in and sat down. Irv motioned to me to notice every official from the Arsenal who had their open briefcases on the table. He was very careful not to smile, but he was delighted when the Judge let go with a tirade about briefcases on the table and watched them scramble to take out the material and bury the cases. They appeared nervous because they felt they got off to a bad start.

The Judge gave instructions and called Bob for his opening statement and reminded him that he was allowed ten minutes. Bob took his legal pad and went to the lectern. I guess he hit on all the right subjects because the judge let him talk for forty-five minutes and never stopped him. He accepted the case. Whew! We were over the first big hurdle. One of the things that Bob said that pleased the judge was, "Your Honor, I promise you at this time that we will make no statements, no accusations, or any claims that we cannot back up with documentation. We will not get into personalities unless the defense brings it up first. We shall concentrate on proving that the Rocky Mountain Arsenal representatives ignored and defied regulations. We are claiming personal and religious prejudice and have proof of every statement we make. I pray you will rule on both counts. Thank you, Your Honor."

For the next two weeks Irv and I drove to the judge's house, parked across the street and sent vibes to His Honor, "Please Judge Habib, rule fairly, that is all we ask." Our lawyer said you are a good judge and a fair man. We know you are Arab and that scares us. Can you be impartial?

We repeated this ritual every day until the decision came through. I thought Irv was going to pass out when he ruled in our favor. Tears came to Irv's eyes – he had been carrying the stress for ten years. He thought it was finally over, but it wasn't.

The Army appealed the decision. The courts denied the appeal and ordered the government to pay Irv $58,000 and to reinstate him in the job he left when he entered the Armed Forces. This money was for the backpay lost through the illegal demotions. Had the courts ruled "religious prejudice" we would have also received the $14,000 we had paid our lawyer.

We sold our little house and with the money we bought a beautiful new big townhouse which we both loved, which I still enjoy to this day.

Sometimes we need to hear, "If you pray to G-d for something and do not get it, remember, 'No' is an answer too."

# Chapter 27
# You Are the Fire

"If you can say you were wrong, you are saying
you are wiser today than yesterday."
– Mama

I was happily sitting in the dark theater, holding Candy's hand on my right and Irv's hand on my left. The movie was a thriller. On the screen, the young single mother was quietly creeping down the stairs, hugging the wall and gripping her son's baseball bat in both hands. The intruder was just turning the corner at the bottom of the stairs when their eyes met. They stood staring at each other, frozen to the spot.

"Honey, I smell something burning."

"I don't smell anything, relax."

"People who smoke do not smell as well as those who do not smoke. I tell you there is a fire nearby."

"Yes, Daddy, I smell something burning, I do!"

Thoroughly disgusted at being distracted at the high point of the story, my husband grumbled, "All right, all right, I'll go get the usher."

"Please do, I am getting nervous and Candy smells it too. I am not crazy."

Our talking disturbed those sitting around us and they started to "SHUSH" us. My daughter and I sat patiently waiting for Irv to get back. We debated about leaving the theater when we saw Irv, the manager and his large flashlight approaching us.

"Mother look, Daddy's jacket is burning!"

I yelled, "Honey, look at your left pocket, your jacket is burning!"

"Daddy! Daddy! YOU ARE THE FIRE!" Several men and the manager were slapping at Irv's jacket, and the manager started to shove him out of the nearest exit. When they were outside everyone around us started to applaud and yell, "HURRAH!"

Outside Irv removed his jacket, and stamped out the fire on the ground. He then emptied the pockets of his personal belongings and threw the jacket into the trash bin. He returned to the seat and made us sit through the movie a second time so that he could see the part he missed.

The next day he bought a new herringbone tweed jacket to replace the burned one and had me sew suede patches on the elbows as I had done before. I couldn't believe my eyes when I saw him put his pipe in the pocket again. I told him to raise his right hand and place his left hand on the Bible and swear, "I, Irv Isaacson, do solemnly swear, that I will always empty the ashes from my pipe before I put my pipe in my pocket."

*Candy, 7 years old, 1948*

# Chapter 28
# The Shvitz

צְדָקָה

*Tzedakah*

Charity — a mainstay of Jewish life

**M**ondays and Thursdays were ladies' days at a Russian bathhouse called The Shvitz. All the poker players gathered with huge lunch sacks to cover lunch, dinner and snacks. The bathhouse was open from 10 AM to 10 PM and the ladies took advantage of every moment. My husband dropped his mother off in the morning and picked her up at night. The women had their first sweat and massage. They were now eating lunch and playing poker. Soon they would stop for a nap. Mrs. Kaminsky, who is 4'8" and overweight, fainted and slid off the chair onto the floor. One of the ladies grabbed a newspaper and began to fan the faintee. Another lady said, "Show her four aces and she'll come to."

After she was revived and moved to a cot, my mother-in-law sat on a chair beside her and said, "You should go to a doctor and see why you fainted."

"I don't have a doctor. I'm never sick."

"Go to see my son, the doctor. He will help you. I'll call my son, Irv, to come take you to the doctor's office." The women helped Mrs. Kaminsky get dressed and she was ready by the time my husband got there. He called his brother's office and told him not to leave because he was on his way with a patient.

Dr. Isaacson escorted Mrs. Kaminsky into his private office. He said, "Mrs. Kaminsky, I hate to tell you this, but you have a bad heart."

The patient became very indignant, swelled up in anger, and said, "I have a bad heart? How can you say that? I give to every charity in Denver!"

# Chapter 29
# The Affair

"אַ ליגנער הערט זײַנע אייגענע ליגנס אַזוי לאַנג, אַז ער גלויבט זיי אַליין."

*"A ligner hert zeyne eygene ligns azoy lang, az er gloybt zey aleyn."*

"A liar hears his own lies so long that he believes them himself."

– Mama

I t has been said that "a husband is someone you should never get smart with 'cause you might be the wife that he's willing to part with."

It was our 15th year of a happy marriage. Irv's hair was showing signs of receding, and he was in shock about it. He was having back problems. I was still a slim thirty-four, twenty-four, thirty-four, the same as on my wedding day. Our daughter Candy was eight years old. Of course there were signals, but I was not looking for them. Usually when a man is having an affair, he picks a fight with his wife so he can slam out of the house angry, like it was her fault. But Irv was not like that.

On Saturday night, around six o'clock, he would take us to Elitch's. We three walked hand in hand through the beautiful, colorful flower garden splashed with bright red, vivid yellows, pretty lavenders and purples. Then Candy would get to go on any ride she wanted, and Irv bought us a hot dog, pop, and an ice cream cone. For some reason he was never hungry, and he didn't have any food. When we were satisfied and tired, we headed home. He dropped us off at the house and went to Lake Steam Baths on Colfax to get relief for his back problem.

One Saturday night I went to a movie with my sister-in-law. I was telling her about poor Irv's back.

"Jean, I am sick and tired of the excuses you always make for your husband. I can't believe you are such a fool. I have debated a long time about telling you this, but I really think you should know. Irv is having an affair. It has been going on for about a year."

My face turned very hot, and my hands turned to ice. I dropped my purse. As I stooped down to pick it up, I thought, one minute the world could be sunshine, the next minute it could become a deep, dark, cold pit. I had been betrayed! "Gert, I guess I really knew but I was in denial. I called the sweat bath several times when he should have been there, but he was not. Do you know who she is?"

"Yes, it's his secretary."

"Oh, that's why he told me that family was not invited to the office Christmas party this year. Of course, she went to a Salt Lake seminar with him! This whole thing is crazy. Nothing has changed in our marriage. He treats me well, he's affectionate, and he is home every night except Tuesdays when he plays Pan, and of course, Saturdays, when he goes to the shvitz. That's a joke. I guess Saturday night dinners, then eight hours a day and lunch hours are enough for him."

Sunday morning, we had the usual bagel and cream cheese with lox and purple onions. We shared the paper. It was funny, we both wanted the same sections. "Go ahead, you take it."

"No, you read it first, I can read something else." A person would think it was an ordinary Sunday morning.

I said nothing to Irv that day. I was in shock. I had a lot to think about. Mama used to say that when you trade one man for another, you simply trade the faults of one man for the faults of another man, so you might as well get used to the faults of the man you've got.

On Monday I put on my best tailored suit and walked into my husband's office at eleven forty-five.

"What a surprise. What are you doing here?"

"I just thought it would be nice if you went to lunch with your wife for a change." He was very nervous. He looked over at his secretary. She got up and walked over to the files. I was simply delighted to see she had an ugly, big shelf on her behind.

Irv couldn't get out of there fast enough. He grabbed his hat and my elbow and said to the room, "I'm going to lunch." When we got off the elevator, he said, "It's your party, where do you want to eat?"

"You can take me to a romantic lunch at the Ship's Tavern at the Brown, or we can be buddies and have a hot pastrami sandwich at Saliman's."

"OK, let's go to the Ship's Tavern."

The downtown street was crowded with shoppers. Irv put his hand on my waist to help guide me through the throng. He took my arm at the crossing, helping me down the curb and across the street. He opened the door to the restaurant and held my chair before he sat down. My heart was pounding, and sour bile was creeping into my throat.

After we ordered, I started, "I know you are having an affair with your secretary, and I know it's been going on for a year. I was waiting for it to end," I lied, since I only found out about it Saturday night. "Or for you to hang yourself, whichever came first. I guess you have hung yourself. You can pack tonight and leave."

Now came the "never admit anything, deny everything line." I swear there are printed instructions or seminars men take, because they all do and say the same thing – deny. Never admit anything. "Who told you that wild tale? It isn't true."

"Stop lying. Really, dear, don't you think you should see a specialist about your back problem? I hate seeing you suffer like that." I gave him no more time to invent stories. I got up and left the restaurant with Irv in hot pursuit. I heard him tell the hostess, on the run, that I was ill, and to cancel our lunch order.

He caught up with me and turned me to face him with both of his hands on my shoulders. "Honestly, Jean, I never meant to hurt you. I never meant to break up our marriage. What I did had nothing to do with us. I promise I will never see her again. It's over, I was a stupid jerk, I love you. Show me a man who can turn it down when it is thrown in his face." All the same old cliches all cheating husbands use.

"Oh, you make me so angry. If I was sleeping with another man, would you buy it if I told you that it had nothing to do with us? And don't use the word 'honestly"because you don't know what it means."

"Jean, I swear, I never slept with her."

"Stop saying that. You make me sick."

"Honey, I promise I will never see her again."

I pulled away from him, "How can you say that when you have

to see her every day at work. Please leave me alone. If you hurry, you still have time to take her to lunch like you usually do." And I walked away.

That evening he tried to talk to me, but I wouldn't listen to anything he had to say, like, "I guess I went crazy...or innocent by reason of insanity."

"I can't believe anything you tell me. I want to confront her to get the true picture. I'll wait in the car. Let's go."

It took him a little while to come out of the house. I knew he was calling her to tell her we were coming, and some instructions, no doubt. As we drove along, I closed my eyes and relived the time we were thirteen years old, and he put the leaf from a lilac bush on my lips and kissed me. That was when we started to go steady. At the time when we were sixteen and he swore to me he would never treat me any differently than he did then. He had kept his word. I recalled the wonderful nights of love making that would never again be the same. When we reached her door, Irv knocked.

"Why are you knocking? I'm sure you have a key."

She let us in and stood in the middle of the room waiting for the onslaught. She didn't invite us to sit. It was a small buffet apartment, clean and furnished as well as a single woman could do on a secretary's pay. There were pretty, fresh flowers on the coffee table and four bright throw pillows on a dull, old couch. I saw a pipe and a large can of Revelation Tobacco on an end table.

"Oh, how cozy, Irv's brand of tobacco." I turned to her and said, "If you want him, you can have him." I spun around and walked quickly out of the door. Irv came right after me. I ran up the street toward the bus line, while my husband got into the car to follow me. He opened the window on the passenger side and kept calling for me to get into the car. I ignored him. He finally parked the car and ran after me. I felt like a fool, standing on the sidewalk arguing, with all the people passing, staring, and laughing, so I got into the car. I sat as far away from him as the seat would allow, looking out of the window away from Irv. Not a word was exchanged all the way home.

Damn, it was hard to hate him. He never, ever forgot anything I asked him to do. He was so damned dependable. I could always depend on him, and I would miss that. If I sneezed, he would jump up for a Kleenex. He was always so aware of everything around him. If I tried to get something out of reach, he was right there to get it for me. It would be pretty hard to replace him.

When he pulled up in front of the house, I opened the car door and ran across the street, toward the lake. He started the car and made a U-turn to follow me. It was dark and I hid behind a large bush. I watched him drive up and down looking for me. Finally, I saw him drive home. It was very quiet, and I heard a twig snap. Was that an animal or a person? Neither idea was welcome. What did I do to deserve this? My every thought was always, "How can I help him, how can I please him, how can I keep him from stress so we could still be together when we get old?" I had to admit he did the same for me. Damn him! It isn't fair! I was cold and I started to know real fear, so I decided I had better head home.

I could see Irv watching out of the front window, so I walked around and slid in the back door. I went directly to the bedroom and undressed. I got into bed without even washing my face. After a while Irv came into the dark room and sat beside me on the bed. He tried to hold my hand, but I jerked it away. "Don't touch me."

"Honey, we have to talk."

"Don't 'Honey' me. There is nothing to talk about. Either you go, or I do."

My husband sighed loud and deep, and said, "Jean, didn't you ever make a mistake? I'll do anything to fix this. You know I love you. Have I ever neglected you or mistreated you? Men are just different from women. We have to think about our daughter."

"Then why didn't YOU think about our daughter? You know, Irv, life has been pretty good to me until now. I really never knew what a real bad hurt was. I never dreamed that pain could be this bad. Remember our philosophy: do anything you want to, as long as you don't hurt anyone else."

"I never meant to hurt you. It was like a game. I was never serious. I know I was a big jerk. You know I never loved anyone but you, ever."

"I'll have to verify that. Please have your secretary send me a memo to that effect."

"Jean, you won't believe this, but I used to tell her all the time that I wished you could be with us. That you were such fun. That we could all three have a ball. I never dreamed it would turn our lives upside down like this." He just kept talking and talking, saying anything that maybe could break me down.

"She had it all figured out. How much child support I would have to pay. You were working so I wouldn't have to pay alimony. We would take Candy every other weekend." He jabbered on and on, again swearing he never slept with her.

"Irv, you would be way ahead if you would shut up. You must have made her feel pretty sure of herself if she was thinking like that. I admit I'm not the smartest woman in the world, but I'm not stupid either. Please, get a pillow and a blanket and sleep on the couch tonight. I don't want to be near you."

"Oh, Honey, don't start that stuff." He ignored me and crawled into bed. He tried to touch me, and I jumped out of bed, grabbed my pillow and a blanket and went into the living room. I curled up on the sofa in the fetal position and went deep inside myself to my secret place where no one else is able to go. I was raw inside. I would not let myself fall apart! You think about the oddest things at a time like that. I remember the day I left a note asking Irv what he would like for dinner, and he had written, "Love." I finally broke down and cried. The sobs and anguish were so deep they would never come out. I thought about whenever he liked the meal he left a tip. It was never big enough to buy a fur coat, but I loved it! I was so mixed up. Every thought was like picking a sore. I cried and sobbed and hiccupped, then finally fell asleep.

I am usually not a crier, but that night I cried myself to sleep. I awoke about four in the morning hoping it was all a horrible dream. Irv was sitting on the floor in front of the sofa, holding my hand and his head in my lap. "Jean, please come back to bed. I can't stand this. You may not think it is possible, but I am hurting more than you are. You don't have the guilt."

"And you don't have the rejected feeling." I started to cry again.

"Please don't cry. I can't stand to see you cry, I know you love me. Say it."

"I am not going to lie and say I don't love you because if I didn't, I wouldn't be in such pain. I always loved you so much because I respected you. Now that is gone, and I feel dead. I always felt so alive when I looked at you, but not today. There is no more color in the world. Everything is gray. I know we fell in love so young that you never had a chance to sow your wild oats. I guess I shouldn't be surprised that this happened. I always thought that you were different, but you are just like all the rest."

"Honey, I swear it will be like it was before. I will fix it. Give me a chance."

I pulled away from him and said, "I used to think you could kiss everything and make it better. But not this. It is beyond fixing."

"Don't say that."

"My father used to tell me that if someone hurt you once, forgive them, it could have been a mistake. If he hurts you a second time, watch out. A third time – that's it. I know this is just once, but that's it. What did I do wrong? Where was I at fault?"

"Don't blame yourself. It was not your fault. I get all the credit. Please don't even think about a separation. Let's both think about our future together. I'll do anything you say. Maybe you will feel better if I bend over and you give me a good, swift kick in the ass. I deserve it."

"Your jokes won't cut it this time. Please go away and let me figure out where I belong."

"You belong with me. We have been so good for each other."

"Irv, there is a price we have to pay for everything we do. I just hope that what you went after gave you enough in return for what you threw away. Go away. All I can think of is how I can hurt you like you hurt me."

"Honey, it is going to be OK. I'll make it OK. Do you want me to bring home BBQ'd ribs for dinner tonight?"

"No! Just go away! I don't care if you never come home for dinner again."

But he didn't leave, and I didn't leave. Could anything be salvaged? It was very quiet around our house for a month. Irv walked on eggshells. His back was miraculously better. He never went to the shvitz. I put on music but never heard it. Every night he tried again to take me in his arms and assure me it was all OK. The "don't-touch-mes" went on. I stayed on the far edge of the bed with my back to him. Slowly, I started to weaken. "Maybe someday I will be able to forgive you, but I will never forget." I was powerless to shake the feeling of desolation. He begged me to "just let it go." Things did start to get a little better as time went on.

He was just like the King in "The King and I." You would want to choke him for some foolish things, and then he would do something wonderful. He was always so proud of me, and that made me feel so good. He was always supportive, no matter how wild my ideas were. "Jeanne's Originals," my dressmaking shop, had all the business in town, but I went broke. He wrote to Washington and got information on how many small businesses went broke, and there were quite a few. That made me feel better. Then there was the Toastmistress speech contest. He said, "Go for it," and I did. Not only did I win, I ended up winning "International." He told the manager at our complex that there wasn't a woman there who could hold a candle to me. How can you stay angry at a man like that?

It took a long time and a thousand "don't-touch-mes" before I started to respond to his playfulness. He tried all the tricks he knew to get me to laugh, and pretty soon he succeeded. I began to heal. I finally admitted to myself that if I did not forgive him, I would miss the Romance of the Century. I was ready to have him on any terms. But it still wasn't fair.

When Candy was a teenager, I asked her why she was always at such odds with her father. She told me "When I was eight years old Daddy took me to his secretary's apartment. We had pancakes, bacon, and ham. Daddy told me not to tell you because you would be angry that we ate ham and bacon." Her relationship with her father was never good after that. Whenever he would correct her, she thought, "Who are you to tell me about right and wrong?"

That was the saddest part about the whole affair. I was always smug and proud because I was not one of those suspicious wives, until I was burned. It is very difficult, if not impossible, to restore trust.

One day I was in a shopping center parking lot putting a large package into the trunk of my car. I saw a small paper sack from one of our better stores. It was a beautifully wrapped small package and a sales check that told me it was an expensive bottle of perfume. If it was on the up and up, why was it hidden in the trunk?

I sat in the living room tapping my foot and becoming angrier by the minute. I heard the back door open, and my husband lingered in the kitchen for a while. When he finally walked into the living room I said, "Who in the hell is the perfume for?" He took my hand and led me to the kitchen. On the counter was a drinking glass filled with water and a lovely single rose in it and the small package I had seen in the trunk of the car. There was a note that read, "I haven't bought you a gift, for no reason at all, for a long time. I love you."

If I ever hated my husband –

# Chapter 30
# Peel Me a Pear

"עס געזונטערהייט."

*"Es gezunterheyt."*

"Eat in good health."

— Mama

My husband received a telephone call from an old friend who lived in Des Moines, Iowa. He needed a favor. It seems that a man in his congregation needed the community's help. He was very ill, had no health insurance, and he needed to come to Denver for medical help. His wife and two grown daughters had kicked him out of the house to shift for himself. The family refused to help him in any way. The congregation had collected enough money for a plane ticket and some cash for daily expenses. "Did we know any family where he could get free board and room for two weeks?"

Candy was away at college and her bedroom was available. Without consulting me, Irv at once offered our home. In all honesty, I wasn't too keen about it, but I went along with my husband's wishes. I guess I could survive two weeks, earn *mitzvah*, and get points for heaven.

When Mr. Boxer arrived, we picked him up at the airport. When it came time to tip the porter, he got lost in the rest room or somewhere. Irv did all the tipping with no "thank yous." When we reached the house, we settled our guest in our daughter's room. I showed him the space in the closet and the two empty drawers. I put a new box of Kleenex out, some paper cups, and clean towels in the bathroom. I turned his bed down and even put a mint on his pillow. I thought it might bring a smile to his lips.

In a few minutes he walked out with a pair of trousers and a shirt over his arm and asked if I would press them for him. He caught me off guard or I would have suggested we drop them at the cleaners in the morning. I went downstairs to the laundry room and pressed the clothes. I returned the things to him with a fresh bar of soap and a couple of books for the bedside table. He followed me out of the room and asked if I had a new toothbrush and toothpaste. I spent the next two weeks waiting on our guest and chauffeuring him from doctor to doctor and hospital to hospital for exams and X-rays.

Whenever we were home, I was at his beck and call and my very helpful, generous husband was getting a little impatient with our guest, because he was such a *chazir,* and with me because I didn't speak up. Of course, he didn't either...

One evening we were sitting and watching TV. Mr. Boxer turned to me and said, not asked, "Peel me a pear, Jean." I looked my husband in the eyes, and he got the message.

I got up from my chair, went into the kitchen and took a plate from the shelf, got a napkin, a fork and a paring knife and a pear. I plopped them down on his lap in such a manner that left no doubt how I felt about the situation. I mumbled, "Is there any wonder his family kicked him out?"

We took him to the airport the next day. He took the box of Kleenex, the toothbrush, and the toothpaste when he left.

From that day forward we referred to him not as Mr. Boxer, but as "peel me a pear."

# Chapter 31
# The Miniskirt

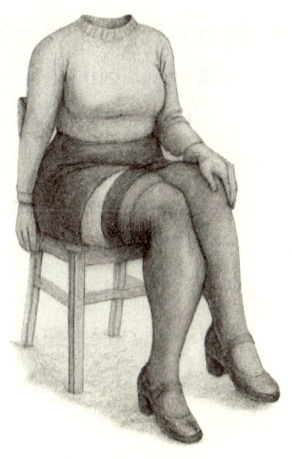

"‏גאָט העלפֿט אונדז!‏"

*"Got helft aundz!"*

"G-d help us!"

— Mama

G-d help us, the miniskirt is back. Ladies, I know you are going to hate me for this, but you've got to admit we can be pretty mule-headed about a lot of things. It doesn't matter what age, shape, or size we are, we want to be "in." We fell in line with the midi, the maxi, the mini, hot pants, the long pants, the bell bottom, the narrow, the straight skirt, the flare, the long hair, the short hair, the pointed, the round, the square toed shoes, and the high, the chunky, and the low heel. The shoe styles changed so fast one year, I gave away twenty-seven pairs of shoes to Goodwill. It is obvious all women are not suited for the same style, but we try.

Do you remember when the miniskirt came out for the first time in 1966? Well, there were two reasons I would not wear a miniskirt. My right leg and my left leg. It was just about then I started to gain weight for the first time in my life. I had a black knit sheath dress that I wore just below my knees, but as I gained weight and got wider in the hips, my dress stretched sideways and got shorter until I was wearing the miniskirt I swore I would never wear.

Big burly Tom's package of cigarettes and the book of matches were rolled in the sleeve of his T-shirt. His big truck rumbled off the highway into the city and he rolled through the congested traffic into the downtown area. He would sure be glad when he got through town and could pull into the truck stop for a relaxing beer.

I was behind the wheel of my car. I was a little overweight, wearing the black knit sheath dress that crept up to the middle of my thighs as I drove. Both the truck and I stopped at a red light alongside each other. I glanced down and saw this really ugly sight. This was in the days before panty hose. The tops of my stockings, the edge of my two-way stretch girdle, the garters and that ugly glob of flesh that protrudes between the girdle and the top of the stocking, were all in plain sight. I looked to my left and to my horror the truck driver was sitting two feet higher than me, and was looking down into my car, enjoying the awful view. I yanked at my skirt trying to pull it down, to no avail. The truck driver laughed and said, "Relax lady, my weakness is liquor."

A survey at a college in Australia showed that hemlines reveal a lot more than just women's legs. They contend that a girl on the hunt wears her skirts the shortest. The girl who has landed a couple of prospects drops her skirt a little. The engaged girl wears hers a little longer, while the newlywed drops hers closer to the top of the knee. But the older woman who is on the hunt lets her skirt fly high again. For those ladies who are up in years, and feel they still have pretty good-looking legs and prefer to flaunt them, you must be prepared for the disappointed looks in the eyes of the beholder as they travel from ankle to thigh to face.

I think that I shall never see
A thing as ugly as a knee
Above whose gnarled and knotted crest
The shorter hemline comes to rest.
Or one that's even worse than that
When it is padded well with fat.
A knee that may in summer wear
Not a thing but be quite bare
Behind whose flex there now remains
A web of blue and broken veins.
Some knees continue to perplex
How can they form the letter X
While in another set one sees
A pair of true parentheses.
Small fools write verses such as these
But greater fools display their knees.

Forty is the old age of youth and fifty is the youth of old age.

# Chapter 32
# The Welcome

"...love your fellow as yourself..."
– Leviticus 19:18

After we had been married thirty years, my "Sunday go to meeting manners" might have slipped a little. I have always loved to work with my hands and would sometimes get carried away, concentrating to the point that I was not aware of what was going on around me. Irv walked into the house and, and without even looking up I grunted a "Hi," and kept working.

He walked over to me and just stood there. "Jean, tell me, how would you greet a friend that came into your house?"

"Well, I guess I would smile, go greet him with a hug and tell him how nice it was to see him again."

"So, don't you think I am entitled to the same treatment?"

I was embarrassed. I got the message, stood up and gave him a kiss and a hug.

"That's much better."

From that day forward, whenever I heard the garage door go up, I would station myself in the hall with my arms outstretched, waiting for him to walk into my embrace. He did the same for me when I came in. We never stopped doing that. What a teacher. That's my guy.

# Chapter 33
# Change of Focus

"When I was young, I admired clever people.
Now that I am old, I admire kind people."
– Jean Isaacson

I was working as a correspondence clerk for the federal government when a new employee came to work in our office. I never was one who put too much stock into good looks. A smile and a good disposition were far more important when you had to spend eight hours a day with a person. Oh, but this was a shocker.

The young woman was well dressed, her auburn curly hair was clean and shiny, but the bones were missing from the left side of her face. I had a very difficult time looking at her when we spoke one on one. I was extremely uncomfortable.

That night at dinner I told Irv about the situation and admitted that it made me sick to my stomach when I looked at her. I felt guilty about it, but those were the facts. As time went by, I found her to be the most pleasant, cooperative and efficient employee I had ever worked with. Nothing was too hard for her to do, and pretty soon they were giving her more and more responsibility, which she accepted gladly. I got to know and appreciate her more each day and soon she was having coffee breaks with the rest of us.

One night Irv asked me how I was managing with the woman I had told him about. "You know, Honey, she is the greatest gal, I just love her, and I don't even notice her deformity anymore."

# Chapter 34
# Rose

"Start to finish the rest of your life."
– Anonymous

S ince the death of her husband two years ago, Rose lived the life of a recluse. She left her house only to get groceries or to see her doctor. Thank goodness, one day she saw the light. She looked into the mirror and yelled at herself, "This is crazy. What are you doing to yourself? You are not helping your dead husband. It was not your fault that he is dead and you are alive. You were a good wife. Start to finish the rest of your life."

The first thing she did was go to the beauty shop and get the works: a haircut, a permanent wave, a facial, a manicure, and a pedicure. Then she went shopping and bought three complete outfits, starting with underwear and finishing with wraps. She then made reservations at a resort hotel. On the plane, Rose closed her eyes and psyched herself up. "I will be aggressive; if nobody talks to me, I will talk to them."

She met some of the ladies around the pool. They hit it off right away. They had lunch together, played bridge all afternoon, and in the evening, they dressed up and went to dinner shows. Rose was having a wonderful time. On the fourth day, she noticed a man she hadn't seen before. No problem, she sauntered over to him and asked, "Did you just get here? I haven't noticed you before."

"Yes," he answered quietly.

"Where are you from?"

"Well-I made up my mind I was not going to lie. I just got out of prison. I have been in prison for twenty years."

"Oh, my goodness, what did you do to be in prison for twenty years?"

"I murdered my wife."

Rose smiled and said, "Oh, so you're single."

# Chapter 35
# Empathy

"אויב איינער גראָבט אַ גרוב פֿאַר עמעצן, פֿאַלט ער אַליין אַרײַן."

*"Aoyb eyner grobt a grub far emetsn, falt er aleyn arayn."*

"If someone digs a pit for somebody, he falls into it himself."

– Papa

Irv was the youngest of three brothers. The oldest, Paul, was a very successful doctor who taught Irv that a twenty-five-cent cigar was much better than the five-cent cigar that he could afford. The middle brother was a lawyer who, from childhood, put Irv down to feed his own ego. Irv fell in love too young and never got his bearings until he was forty years old. To prove that he was OK, he became a gadget man. This meant that when he bought a car it had to come fully equipped with everything electrical: sunroof, white walls, spoke hub caps, reclining seats, and a tape deck. In our house he had a TV in every room but the bathrooms, and a telephone in every room, including the bathrooms. He could never admit that he couldn't afford anything if I wanted it.

I tried to convince him that he was the most successful of the three brothers because he had a good marriage while they didn't. He had principles, empathy, a good heart, a wonderful sense of humor, and an extreme sense of fairness. I used to call him "the last angry man" because he flew into a rage at injustice. He protected anyone who needed protection, he helped anyone who needed help no matter what obstacles he had to overcome to do what was necessary. He used to say, "That selfish bastard has a loaf of bread under each arm, and he condemns the man that simply wants a slice of bread."

We were in a supermarket one day and Irv noticed a young mother with a six-month-old baby. In her cart there was bread, butter, milk, and noodles. She was counting her change and studying the things in the cart to decide which thing to put back on the shelf. Irv walked up to her and handed her a ten-dollar bill. She started to cry and refused the money but then relented and asked for his name and address to pay him back when she could.

"No, no, you don't pay me back; you help someone in trouble when you can. Pass it on. I kidded him and asked him if it was an ugly fat woman would he have done the same as he did for the pretty young thing. "Yes, I would. That's my way of thanking G-d because I have the extra ten dollars."

Irv worked with a man whose son had a terminal illness, and the financial burden became intolerable. His co-worker cracked under the strain, and he ended up in the hospital with a nervous breakdown. This happened during the time that Denver had the longest cold-spell I can remember. Irv asked me if I had any old rugs, blankets, bedspreads, bathmats or anything he could use. He cautioned me not to expect to get them back. He went to the service station and bought some antifreeze. He drove over to Kennedy's house and found his old car on the street as he expected. He got warm water from a neighbor and poured it over the radiator until the ice melted, and he could drain it. After he put the antifreeze into the car, he covered the motor with all the things I had given him and anchored them down with stones and bricks, so they could not blow away. When he got home, he explained, "That's all Kennedy would need is to come home to a car with a cracked block; it would send him back over the edge."

During the war, Irv was an instructor at Lowry Field. He called me one day and said he was bringing home a soldier for dinner. I knocked myself out to make it a special home cooked meal: salad, brisket, mashed potatoes, asparagus tips, apple sauce, then peach pie a la mode. When the meal was over the young Italian soldier pushed his chair back, patted his stomach and gave me the highest compliment, "Mrs. Isaacson, you couldn't buy this meal in a restaurant for a dollar seventy-five." This became a family joke. Whenever we had an exceptionally good meal, everyone would sing out in unison, "Mrs. Isaacson, you couldn't buy this meal in a restaurant for a dollar seventy-five."

~

Our friends used to say, "When Jean sneezes, Irv jumps up for a Kleenex." He did want me to have anything I wanted, and I was careful not to want too much. I always worked and kept the pressure off him as much as I could. I wanted him to stay healthy so he would be with me when we were old. Despite his generosity, the first three months of every year I was asked to "cool it" because all the big bills came due then. I tried my best not to spend money during that period. One year, in October, I put a black knit suit in "Will Call" and ordered a black fox collar and cuffs from Canada, through the Denver Dry Goods.

On January 16th I received a call from the store telling me to come pick up my fur. It came packed in a beautiful large box. Just my luck, Irv called and said he would pick me up after work and we would go to dinner.

At coffee break I told my friends my dilemma. The janitorial service was accused of stealing at night, so I was afraid to leave the package overnight. My friend suggested that I put the fur into an old supermarket sack and when I got into the car to just "throw" the bag into the back seat as though it were nothing important. I did it and it worked. A month later I got the black suit out of "Will Call," put the collar and cuffs on it and showed Irv the wonderful bargain I got, showing him the sales check for the suit only. He agreed it was a great price. No problem. About ten years later I told this story at a party. It was the first time my husband had ever heard it, and he was livid. I don't think I have ever seen him so angry at me. He hated it because I had lied to him. He didn't speak all the way home.

When we got in the house, accusations flew in all directions about who told more lies to whom. When things calmed down, Irv got a magazine with a picture of the Mona Lisa and told me that it is exactly how I look when I didn't believe what he said. Yes, we made up before we went to sleep. I told his picture the other day: "I don't mind being alone, but I do mind not being with you."

# Chapter 36
# The Dog House

"אויב דו ליבסט לעבן, פארשווענד נישט די צייט. דערפון איז עס געמאכט."

*"Aoyb du libst lebn, farshvend nisht di tseyt. Derfun iz es gemakht."*

"If you love life, don't squander time. That is what it is made of."

— Mama

I am really ashamed of myself, and my entire sex. We created a horrific monster, the Dog House. It is a place where a woman keeps her man when he has violated her rules of domesticity. There isn't a man alive who hasn't occupied it. What is the Dog House? It is a cold, frigid place that has many entrances but only one exit. Her poor guy gets out only when she decides that he can.

Women differ in many ways, but they are all exactly alike as sentinels at the lone door of the Dog House. She has plenty to say with the first barrage, when all hell breaks loose and the sparks fly, but then comes the hardest blow to bear, "THOSE SILENT STARES."

Many times, he wished she would shut up, but when he has been incarcerated long enough, he will welcome a good bawling out.

When my man was in the Dog House, I wore an invisible sign that read, "TEMPORARILY OUT OF ARDOR."

During our lean years, Irv and I talked it over and decided that until our financial picture improved, we would limit our gifts to each other strictly to necessities.

So when his birthday rolled around, I bought him the much-needed fertilizer for our lawn. That evening some friends came over for a potluck birthday supper. A sweet young thing asked my husband, "What did Jean get you for your birthday?"

In an uncalled for, loud voice, he answered, "A pile of manure." Well, there went the party for me and into the Dog House went hubby. For the rest of the week, I spoke over his head to anyone present, just as though he wasn't there. "The SILENT STARE" reigned.

About the easiest way for a man to get into the Dog House is to insult the little woman's vanity. Face it, ladies, as men see it, they never show the ravages of age the way their wives do. With a few drinks under his belt, in his mind he is still the young, virile stud to the bitter end.

Just picture me on the morning when I go to the beauty shop. I am putting up the coffee wearing a worn-out robe and slippers that I thought the big sport was going to replace last *Chanukah*. I admit, I'm twenty pounds overweight, but then so is he.

In the kitchen doorway stands Irv in his bare feet, pajama bottoms, a tee shirt with a hole in the front, a little pot, he needs a shave, his eyes are puffed and his hair, what's left of it, is standing on end, but with typical "MALE EGO" he sings, "THERE SHE GOES, MISS AMERICA."

I ask you, is that a candidate for the Dog House?

As the days went by, I started to worry. Was I dragging the Dog House thing on too long? After all, I did love the guy despite all the awful things I said about him.

Remember, your man is patiently waiting and watching for his way out. Come on, ladies, life is too short, that's no place for man or beast.

"GO HOME AND LET HIM APOLOGIZE."

# Chapter 37
# So Many Good Days

"אַזוי גייט עס."

*"Azoy geyt es."*

"That's how it goes." That's life, generally followed by a deep sigh.

— *Bubbe*

I t was a very hot, humid day…one in which I wouldn't want to be running errands. I was comfortable in the air-conditioned house. It was five o'clock, just the time Irv always came home. He came in all sweaty and worn out. I said, "Honey, you look awful. What's wrong?"

He answered, "This has got to be the worst day of my life. Look at my thumb with the blue fingernail. I slammed it in the car, and it has been killing me all day. Then I had a flat tire and missed a very important appointment. My car door was acting up and I stopped in the service department at Ralph Schomp's and it's going to cost a bundle to fix. I don't know whether it's time to trade it in on a new one or fix it. Then I had to run around to four different Walgreens until I found the exact lipstick you asked me to get. Man, it was hot today."

He then took two aspirins and a long shower. He came out of the bathroom smiling. He said to me, "Jean, we have so many good days coming to us in a lifetime, and so many bad days. Well, I just had one of my bad days so that's one less bad day I have coming."

I can't help but mention that most husbands would have said, "On top of all my problems today I had to run all over town for your blankety blank lipstick." He didn't say that. He was nice.

# Chapter 38
# Thanksgiving 1987

"Who will feed us meat?"
– Leviticus 11:4

Thanksgiving family dinner was at my house every year because I had the largest dining room. As I got older it became difficult to prepare the entire meal for sixteen people all by myself. I called the women and explained the problem. Everyone was anxious to help. My sister Lil would bring the hors d'oeuvres. Ethel would bring her famous fresh cranberry, orange, and nut mold. Uncle Sol bought good dinner rolls from King Soopers. Rose would bring the green vegetables, Belle baked the sweet potatoes, and Goldie baked the pies. Mike owned a bar, so he handled the drinks. Great!

After I stuffed the turkey, Irv took over the job of baking it. We opened the table to seat twelve, and the children were to eat at the bridge table in the den. Everyone liked that arrangement.

There was one real problem. Three of the guests wanted a wing every year and someone was always disappointed. This year Irv had a little secret. He bought an extra wing. Each one of the women who wanted a wing got one. We were all oblivious to the big joke. Since nobody noticed, Irv was deflated.

After dinner as we sat around talking in the living room, Irv was bursting with his secret and he asked, "Well, which one of you lucky ladies got a wing this year?"

Ethel said, "I had one."

Shirley said, "I ate one."

My sister Lil said, "You both couldn't have had a wing because I got one."

Irv said, "How could that be? Three of you claim you got a wing, and the dumb turkey only has two wings. I think one of you ladies should get checked out for Alzheimer's."

Voices were raised. The women started to argue about which one was crazy. Each one was certain she was the sane one. The argument lasted a good half hour and Irv had his fun. He never admitted to anyone, even me, that he baked an extra wing. Every Thanksgiving the argument continues, while Irv laughs in heaven.

I hate the guys
who criticize
and minimize
the other guys
whose enterprise
has made them rise
above the guys
who criticize.

# Chapter 39
# **The Mother of Girls**

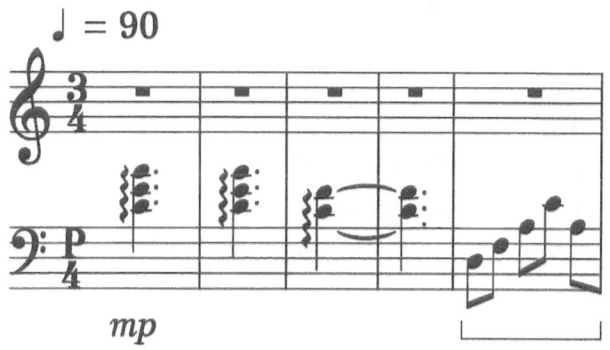

"יִשְׂמֵךְ אֱלֹהִים כְּשָׂרָה, רִבְקָה, רָחֵל, וְלֵאָה."

*"Yismech Elohim ksara, rivka, raḥel, v'le'a."*

"May G-d make you like Sarah, Rebecca, Rachel, and Leah."

– Sabbath blessing for girls

As I was riding along in traffic, I heard Perry Como's *The Father of Girls* on the car radio. The lyrics really got my attention because I was the mother of a girl. The first thing I did when I got home, even before I removed my jacket or shoes, was write a letter to Perry. I explained that not only was I the mother of a girl, but I was also an entertainer. My audiences were very often mothers and grandmothers, and I knew they would relate to the theme. After a week went by, I started to hound the mailbox. On the eighth day I received a large envelope with sheet music of the song and a short note wishing me good luck, written and signed by Perry Como. Bless his heart!

For me, the lyrics would be:

*When you're the mother of boys,*
*How you worry.*
*But when you're the mother of girls,*
*You do more than that, you pray.*
*From the time of the diaper and pin,*
*Till the time she cries, "Don't come in."*
*Till the time you gown her in white*
*And give her away*
*You worry, you worry, night and day.*
*When she's a plain little girl,*
*How you worry.*
*But when she's a beautiful thing*
*You do more than that, you pray.*
*Boys come round when they want a date*
*Girls may only sit home and wait.*
*When she's out, you sit up all night.*
*With her first baby curl*
*You trust her, but you worry*
*Because you were once a girl.*

This reminds me of the three Jewish women sitting around the condominium pool.

Betty, formerly Becky, said, "*OY VEY!*"

Sally, formerly Sarah, said, "OH, DEAR G-D."

Irene, formerly Ida, said, "I thought we weren't going to talk about our children."

If you try to do something and fail, you are much better off than if you try to do nothing and succeed.

# Chapter 40
# A Sunday Drive

"Joy is not in things; it is in us."
– Richard Wagner

Most Sunday mornings, when the weather allowed, we took a leisurely drive into the mountains and found a pleasant place to have breakfast. As we drove along, I carefully suggested to my husband that he might be driving just a little too fast for a mountain road. He glanced into the rear-view mirror and with a frightened look on his face he said, "There is a police car following us. No, don't turn around. Look straight ahead. I am going to make a run for it."

"Are you crazy? I can't believe this. Please slow up, Honey, you are frightening me." When we reached the crest of the hill, Irv swerved the car onto a dry, dirt farm road. With the dust flying behind us, he pulled behind a small barn and cut off the motor. My heart was pounding and neither one of us dared to take a breath. I gave him a wifely disgusted look.

"I am sure the police can see the cloud of dust we left behind. That was the most imbecilic, moronic stunt. I can't believe that an intelligent sixty-eight-year-old man could pull such a dangerous stunt. I guess I was expecting too much from you. You will never grow up. Women are so much smarter than men. No woman on earth would ever try a dumb thing like that. It would serve you right if we both ended up in jail; then who would bail you out? My big shot husband, the criminal." Irv

*Irv and Jean strolling in City Park on their 40th wedding anniversary, 1978*

got out of the car very quietly; careful not to slam it, he closed the door. He crept along the barn wall, western movie style, and peered cautiously around the corner. "There they go up the highway. Good, we have lost them."

He got back into the car and saw the black look on my face. He burst out laughing. Darn him, there never was a police car. He was pulling my leg. After fifty years of marriage, I still could not tell when he was serious or joking. There was never a dull moment with that guy.

# Chapter 41
# So, You Are Sixty-Five Years Old

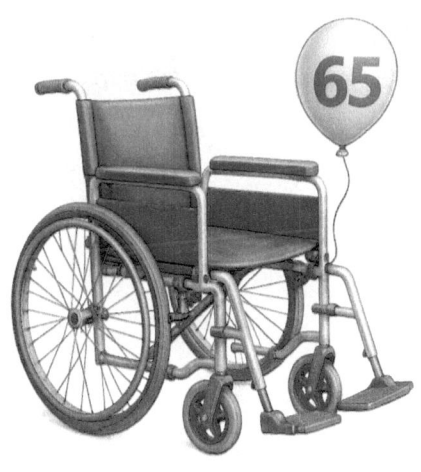

"A bore is someone who deprives you of
solitude without providing you with company."
– Oscar Wilde

On Irv's sixty-fifth birthday, he would finally get his Social Security. I decided it was sort of special, and we would have a surprise birthday for him. That would be the day that you could ever fool my husband. He told me he would be late for dinner. He explained that he had a business appointment, and he would get home at about eight o'clock. That was perfect. I would have plenty of time to get everything ready and have all the guests hidden in the bedroom when he got home.

Everyone parked their cars down the street and were all in place when the doorbell rang at eight o'clock. I answered the door and found Irv in a wheelchair, in his bathrobe with an ice bag tied to his head. Pushing the wheelchair were two topless nurses, with caps in place. I called everyone out of the bedroom to view the big surprise. That got the party off to a great start. I got a couple of sweaters, and we invited the topless nurses to join the party.

The rental of the wheelchair and the cost of the girls totaled two hundred and fifty dollars, and he thought it was worth it.

# Chapter 42
# Lovers to the End

"It is written that a Jewish husband should see his aging wife
just as he saw her when she came to him as a young bride.
HA – that'll be the day!"
– Jean Isaacson

We were both seventy-two years old and had just celebrated our fifty second wedding anniversary. We lived in a townhouse complex of one hundred and sixty-seven units, in clusters of four. The unit next to ours changed hands and, just my luck, the new owner was a young divorcee in her early forties. I had not yet met her. One day I was fixing the salad when I heard the garage door open and Irv's car drove in. After about fifteen minutes passed and he still wasn't in the house. I peeked into the garage and found the door was open, the car was there, but the husband wasn't.

After a while Irv came into the house and told me that our new neighbor had asked if he had a tall ladder because the light bulb in her garage had burned out. Like a good neighbor, he took the ladder, climbed up, and changed the bulb for her.

About three days later the same thing happened again, but this time he was gone for forty-five minutes. It seems the chain on her automatic garage door opener was off track. My big macho husband, who would have called in the garage-door people to fix ours rather than get all greasy, fixed it for her with a smile.

The following week was a repeat, but this time it was a delay of one hour and fifteen minutes. This time it seems she had ordered a table, and it was delivered unassembled, and the sweet thing just didn't know how to do it. Could he please help? I recalled the day my husband told me, "Never, never buy anything that has to be assembled because I will return it before I go through the hassle of putting A with X, missing screws, and needing hot glue." I referred to our new neighbor as the "Phantom" because I still had not seen her. I finally figured out that when I was outside, she stayed in, but when Irv was there, out she popped. Well, getting a husband is one thing, and keeping him is another. I started to be concerned.

I was sitting under the dryer in the beauty shop, looking through the current Cosmopolitan when I came across an article entitled, "What is sex appeal?" It listed twenty items. Number one was a pretty smile – I don't know how pretty mine is, but I do smile a lot. I passed that one. Number two was a nice perfume – and I had some of that. Number three was black velvet slacks – I had a pair hanging in my closet. They were too small, but I had them, so I counted them. Painted toenails – I still had the remnants of my pedicure from last July in Las Vegas. You know, one-fourth inch of polish left on the big toe, so I passed that one too. I went clear through number eleven, and I had a perfect score when I came to black sheer nighty. I hadn't owned a black sheer nighty since I wore out the one in my trousseau.

I grabbed my trusty charge-a-plate and dashed down to the May Company, now Foley's. Just as though an angel had its arms around me, there, on a reduced rack, hung a black sheer peignoir set, just my size, large, originally one hundred and fifty-five dollars, on sale for half price.

That night I fixed Robert his favorite dinner. His name was really Irv, but I called him Robert Redford because he looks just like the actor under the arms and elbows. When he came home, I met him at the door with a big smile and a kiss. While he was at his desk going through the mail, I brought him a tall, cold glass of iced tea. He left a tip after dinner, something he always did when he liked the meal. I puffed the pillow on the couch, brought him the paper, untied his shoes and slipped them off. It was a hot day, and his damp socks were stuck to the bottoms of his feet, so I pulled the socks away from the soles of his feet and he said, "Ah." I smiled, smiled, smiled. The stage was set.

I went into the bedroom and slipped into my latest purchase. I put a dab of his favorite Opium perfume behind each ear and on my wrists. Try to picture this – seventy-two years old, twenty-five pounds overweight, forget about the cellulite, and enough veins to go to a masquerade party in the nude as a road map. I sauntered into the living room. Robert sat upright, his eyes popping, he gave me the old wolf whistle that I hadn't heard in years. He reached toward me, took hold of the price tag hanging from the sleeve, and said, "SEVENTY-SEVEN DOLLARS AND FIFTY CENTS!"

Two rabbis were discussing the forthcoming marriage of Marilyn Monroe and Arthur Miller. Says one, "Ah, I don't give it a year."

Replies the other, *"Aza yor zol ikh hobn."* (Such a year I should have.)

## Chapter 43
# Nothing Could Be Finer

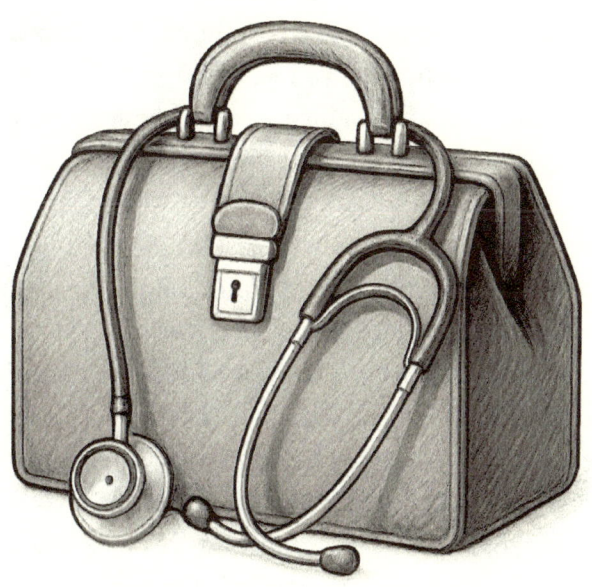

"If everybody on the block put their bundle of troubles in a big pile,
they'd all grab their own bundle and run home with it."
– Mama

Irv was always there for anyone who needed him. Nothing took too much energy or too much time. If he could afford it, it would be done. In fact, the very first time I noticed that he was not himself was when we were visiting his brother, Paul, in Tucson. Paul was recovering from a stroke and had enough money to pay for any kind of help, so he got used to expecting anyone around to be at his beck and call. Every time Irv sat down, Paul would ask for something. It got to the point that I heard Irv groan every time Paul called his name. He did what he was asked but he was getting pretty disgusted with his brother. He started to go into the bedroom to take naps three or four times a day. This was not like him at all. He was always ready to run and go and do. I started to jump up to spare Irv whenever Paul called him.

When we came back to Denver, Irv hired a handyman to help him hang the plants on the patios. I saw him raise his arm to point and he could hardly get his arm up above his shoulder. I went out to help and he spoke sharply to me, "I'm not a cripple." He was getting sensitive about his diminished strength, and I knew it was time to go to the doctor.

The doctor said, "Irv, this is April. Your blood count is half what it was when I examined you in November." I said, "Doctor, please refer us to a specialist to whom you would send your mother, your wife, or your daughter if they had a blood disorder."

The specialist had a very small unpretentious office, staffed by one girl. He saw us right on time. He was about forty years old, not more than five foot two, and very thin. He was neat and clean, but his suit was a cheap polyester, right off the rack, and obviously never tailored because the sleeves and pants were a little long. He carried a King Soopers plastic bag, folded over to fit the contents. It appeared to be his lunch. We both thought, "I hope his rent is paid."

Dr. Finer studied the records we brought with us. He said, "Irv, you go check into Rose Hospital right now. I will leave orders for the blood work. Mrs. Isaacson, you go home and bring Irv whatever he needs."

We learned very quickly that this wonderful, mild mannered, quiet man suffered greatly for his terminally ill patients. We always knew when the news was bad because his right leg jumped up and down very rapidly as he spoke. No bedside manner, no flowery speeches, just the true ugly facts. He watched over Irv just as though he was his own child.

Dr. Finer studied the charts, the medical books, explained, watched, and worked what seemed to us twenty-four hours a day, while his patient chilled, fevered, and vomited.

After the second horrible chemotherapy session, he suggested to Irv and me that we go on a nice vacation, perhaps on a cruise. Of course, we knew what that meant. However, Irv loved his home, and he decided he would rather be home. We laughed a lot and thanked G-d for our five years of courtship and fifty-two years of marriage, love, and fun.

Even though Dr. Finer was unable to save my husband's life, when it was all over, I felt like, "G-d, move over and let Dr. Finer sit down."

## Chapter 44
## Six Weeks to Remember:
## 8/26/97 to 10/8/97

"מען פּלאַנירט, אֲדוֹנָי לאַכט."

*"Men planirt, Adonai lakht."*

"Man plans, G-d laughs."

– Mama

At 10:45 A.M. on August 26th, I left my writing group. I was content, buzzing along in my car on the newly widened Alameda Avenue. When I reached Monaco, I turned south to visit my daughter. As I approached Leetsdale I noticed flashing lights behind me. Never dreaming the lights were intended for me, I pulled over and parked.

To my surprise the police car stopped behind me. The officer walked up to my window and lectured me about the children sitting on the grassy median strip on Alameda. I assured him that I'd noticed them. He went on about driving sixty miles an hour in a thirty-five mile an hour zone. I would have to go to the night traffic court. I told him that I was eighty and didn't feel good about walking and parking in the dark, downtown, by myself. He repeated that it was a serious violation and night court would be needed. I accepted the ticket quietly. He drove off while I sat there inhaling deeply, unable to believe I had been traveling sixty. I remembered I had just had my car serviced and made a mistake at the pump and put in super octane gas. Maybe that was why my car ran away from me?

Oh dear, couldn't I go to the daytime traffic court? I waited a week. The following Monday I had coffee and bagel at Einstein's, drove downtown, and parked in a lot. I folded three dollars and slipped them into the impossible slots and added fifty cents – the total amount for the day. Finally, the door opened to the Traffic Violation Department where I was told by the clerk that my driving record was not yet in the computer. "Try again in two weeks."

When I reached the parking lot, thirty minutes after I paid for a full day, I noticed a woman trying to dig out the right amount of money. I said to her, "I just paid for a full day only a half hour ago. I'm pulling out of 41, you can save $3.50." I pulled out of 41 and she pulled in. We smiled and waved. We had beaten the system.

When I got home, I noticed I was very short of breath and my ankles were the size of cantaloupes.

On September 16th, I repeated the whole thing, from the bagel and coffee, to "the records are still not here," to cheating the parking lot by giving my space to another poor *shnook*.

By now I was flopping down on my bed very often and found myself short of breath after minimal exertion. I started to refuse invitations and canceled dates. I called my daughter's heart doctor and was told to come right in. I was examined and given an echocardiogram, then sent to register at the hospital. "Come back here at five o'clock tomorrow morning." They would remove fluid from the bag around my heart.

I went home and put the three Cornish hens back into the freezer, called my friends who were invited to lunch and canceled. Next, I packed a bag for my hospital stay.

Candy met me at the hospital the next morning, wished me well, kissed me and said, "Mother, I love you and I need you. If you die, I'll kill you." We both laughed.

The fluid that was removed was blood. This meant cancer or TB. We knew TB was very rare so it couldn't be that. My blood pressure was 240/90 so Dr. Prager was scared to death. They injected medication into the intravenous tube and my pressure started to drop. Whew!

Now they scheduled all kinds of tests to figure out where the blood was coming from. Something else was going on. They scheduled a procedure to put a scope down my throat. No food or drink until after the test. The procedure did not take place until 4:30 P.M. By then I had starved for two days. Do you think I lost an ounce? No!!

My blood test showed the liver numbers were too high, or too low, I don't know which. I'm a gagger and really dreaded the procedure. To make a long story short, I sat there telling the nurses all my latest jokes, then woke up in my room, and didn't remember anything, so I had worried for nothing. They found an obstruction in the liver duct, either a gall stone or a diverticulum. They did a CAT scan of my stomach and chest. This doctor had a family emergency, so I had to wait until the twentieth for my visit with him about the results.

Then to the oncologist for a biopsy of the sack and lining of the heart. I tested positive for TB. The doctor assured me I was not contagious but everyone in the family in Denver and Longmont got tested. Thank G-d they were all OK. Just think, if my grandson, the orthopedic surgeon, was positive, his career as a surgeon would have been over. In addition to my high blood pressure pills (2), my heart pills (2), aspirin (2), and asthma puffs and medication, I have to be on seven TB pills a day for nine months, until June 1998. Oh yes, and 6 vitamins a day. Gag.

I was released from the hospital on the sixth of October. If I didn't appear in court on the seventh a warrant would be issued. Ye Gads, I was almost a criminal.

On the morning of October seventh, I jumped out of bed, bagel and coffee at Einstein's, $3.50 for parking, back to the traffic court clerk. "I'm so sorry. There is no court this morning. There are no judges on duty. If you come back at four fifteen, I will see what I can do to get you taken early so you can get home before dark." I went home, rested until three, came back downtown, and put $3.50 into the parking slot for the fifth time. The clerk was very sweet. She ran all over the building to find the clerk of the court and said it was all taken care of, to go sit down in the hall until the court started at five. There was a room full of traffic offenders.

The Judge called out "Jean Isaacson." I walked to the lectern. The Judge started to speak. "Mrs. Isaacson, I wish to commend you. In all my years on the bench I have never seen such a record. Accolades to you. Fifteen years of an absolutely spotless driving record. What do you have to say?"

"Thank you, your honor. I don't know what happened. I had no idea I was traveling that fast. I was not in a hurry. I have no excuse. If the officer says I was going sixty miles an hour in a thirty-five mile per hour zone, I have to accept that. I'm aware I could plea bargain for less points because of my good driving record, but I can't come back to do that. I leave myself in your hands and assure you this will never happen again." You would have thought we were old chums.

The Judge said, "I know these things do happen." My fine was $38.00 plus costs, a total of $68.00. I got home before dark.

My grandson came into my bedroom later that evening, sat at the foot of my bed and said, "I have talked to all of your doctors. The good news is that you don't have anything you didn't have before, when you were actively bombing around town, going to classes and lunches. The other things can be helped. So, don't lie down and say to yourself, 'I'm eighty years old and sick, just resting and waiting to die.' You do everything the doctor says and go back to accepting invitations, attending classes and doing your One-Woman Shows."

Sunday, I started to have a little pity party and slipped into a blue funk. I was walking into Safeway and saw my reflection in the glass, sagging stomach, rounded shoulders, head forward on my chest with down lines on my face. "No!! That's not me! Stomach in, shoulders back, head up and smile." I did them all, I looked better, and I felt better.

Decisions – should I tell my friends about the positive TB test results? My doctor gave me a letter saying I was not contagious – but would they eat anything I cooked? Would anyone ever hug me again? I'm not afraid to die and you can be sure I'm going to live, really live, 'till I die. I have a show scheduled for November 6th. I laughingly told the woman to call me a few days before the scheduled date to see if I'm still alive.

I plan to see the year 2000.

So nice to meet you – here, let me give you my card.

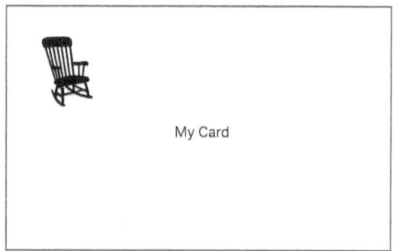

My Card

# Chapter 45
# Candy

"Life only gives you time and space. It's up to you to fill it."
– Jean Isaacson

Candy, gosh, it is hard to believe she is fifty-five years old. And I still worry about her. I could write a book about the worrying and the praying I did when she was overweight at ten. Oh yes, and the period when she had a very serious crush on a Christian boy.

They say, "Little children, little troubles, big children, big troubles."

Now that my daughter is older and her two sons are successful in the adult world, she has become my "mother hen." She worries about me. She checks on me. She advises me. She is lovingly trying to be my mother and I am lovingly resisting.

At age eighty I am my own boss for the very first time in my life. Yes, I still worry about my daughter, my two grandsons, and their wives, and my new great-grandbaby.

Worrying isn't all that bad. It means I am part of a family. What's so bad about that?

*Jean, Irv and Candy on Candy's 21st birthday, 1963*

# Chapter 46
# Rindercella

*This little story was first delivered to the Air Force Academy
Officers' Wives' Club along with her award-winning story, "The
Dog House," on October 26, 1967.*

I t's time for spoonerism. For those of you who don't know what spoonerisms are, I'll explain. For instance, some <u>thinkle</u> might <u>peep</u> they are only for <u>kittle lids</u>, but <u>fiddle</u>-<u>age</u> <u>molks</u> laugh too.

I'm going to tell you the <u>tairy fale</u> about <u>Rindercella</u>, As the <u>thot plickens</u>, it will make your <u>cresh fleep</u> and give you <u>poose gimples</u>. <u>Rindercella</u> lived in a big <u>hark douse</u> with her mean old <u>mepstuther</u> and her two <u>sisty uglers</u> who were very <u>dill</u> and <u>lustless</u>. They made <u>Rindercella</u> do all the <u>wirdy dirk</u> while they just sat around on their <u>fig bannies</u> with their <u>heet</u> in the <u>fair krinking doffee</u>, <u>cheating awklets</u>, and <u>magin readazines</u>.

They were so lazy they wouldn't even put on their own <u>oderam deunderant</u>. One day, <u>Rindercella</u> was in the kitchen <u>flopping</u> the <u>moor</u> when the two <u>sisty uglers</u> came in and said, "the <u>pransom hince</u> is having a <u>bancy fess drall</u>, but you can't go. Now, ain't that a <u>shirty dame</u>?"

<u>Rindercella</u> was <u>tit</u> to be <u>fide</u> and she went back to work with <u>ears</u> in her <u>ties</u>. She was just about to <u>chickazee</u> a <u>fricken</u> when there was a <u>flinding bash</u> of light and standing before her was a <u>feautiful bairy</u>. "I am your <u>mairy fodguther</u>. Now you <u>tie</u> your <u>drears</u> because you are <u>boing</u> to the <u>gall</u>." <u>Rindercella</u> said "I can't go! I have to <u>dawsh</u> the <u>wishes</u> and look at my <u>firty dingernails</u>." Then the <u>mairy fodguther</u> waived her <u>wagic mond</u> and instantly <u>Rindercella</u> was <u>franstormed</u> into a <u>bavishing reauty</u>. She wore a long white <u>gownless</u> evening <u>strap</u> and a necklace of <u>pubies</u> and <u>rearls</u>. On her feet were two tiny <u>slass glippers</u>. The <u>sairy fed</u>, "Remember the <u>stagic will mop</u> when the <u>strock clucks</u> 12."

When <u>Rindercella</u> <u>kit</u> the <u>hastle</u>, that's "hit the castle," she saw <u>ducks</u> and <u>doochesses</u> <u>byling</u> and <u>smowing</u> and the <u>pransom hince</u> said, "May I <u>dave</u> <u>this hance</u>? You are so pretty you remind me of <u>Beeping Slooty</u>." He was just about to ask for her <u>mair</u> in <u>handage</u> when the <u>strock clucked</u> 12 and <u>Rindercella</u> <u>ban</u> from the <u>rall</u>. Oh, wasn't that a <u>shirty dame</u>?

As she ran one of her <u>slass gippers</u> <u>flipped</u> from her <u>soot</u> and the <u>pransom hince</u> <u>pooped</u> to <u>stick</u> it up. "All I <u>dotta goo</u> is <u>gind</u> the <u>firl</u> who <u>sopped</u> this <u>dripper</u> and I'll find my <u>buture fried.</u>" So, they went from house to house (you can't turn that around) to try to <u>gind</u> the <u>firl</u> the shoe fit. Oh yea! It says "shoe fit."

<u>Sitty prune</u> they came to the house where <u>Rindercella</u> lived. They <u>docked</u> on the <u>noor</u>. Who should <u>dome</u> to the <u>coor</u> but the <u>hady</u> of the <u>louse</u>. The two <u>sisty uglers</u> <u>shyed</u> on the <u>troos,</u> but their <u>finky steet</u> were <u>boo tig</u>. And ha ha, wasn't that a <u>shirty dame</u>?

Then, <u>wess gut</u>? <u>Rindercella</u> tried and the <u>flipper pitted</u> <u>serfectly</u>. The <u>hince</u> was so <u>frappy</u> they shot off a 21-<u>sum galoot</u> and played the <u>bum and droogle</u> corps. The <u>coving lupple</u> <u>hissed</u> and <u>kugged</u> and they didn't make out until they <u>mot garried</u> because there was <u>po nill</u> then.

# Chapter 47
# The Mandle Broyt Bake-Off

"דו ווייסט ווי אזוי צו מאַכן אַ מענטש משוגע!"

*"Du veyst vi azoy tsu makhn a mentsh mshuge!"*

"You know how to drive a person crazy!"

– Bam

When our first grandson, Steve, started to talk, he could not say "Grandma," and I became "Bama." It was shortened to "Bam," and Bam I have remained.

When the little boys came to visit or sleep over with Bam and Papa, they would head straight for the old crock full of *mandle broyt* (almond bread). They are now fourteen and sixteen years old, and they still do. What a big disappointment when the crock is empty.

Steve always brought his homework or got busy with something. Whenever I was baking, Ron would sit on the kitchen counter and watch me. One day, Ron said to me, "Bam, could I try to bake *mandle broyt* so the tradition will not be lost?"

We decided to each bake a separate batch and have a *mandle broyt* bake-off. We planned to put a cookie in a plastic bag with a number attached so that the people voting would not know whose cookie they were tasting. Ron was number one, and I was number two. A ballot was attached to the two bags requesting block number one or two be checked, signature, and comments.

The votes started coming in. I was flabbergasted! Ron was winning seven to one. Even Irv and Candy voted for number one. Then Irv's sister-in-law, Aunt Ethel, came in and voted. That made the score seven to two. Ron really felt bad because he thought his precious Bam's feelings were hurt. He comforted me by saying, "Please don't feel insulted. If you lose, it only means you were a good teacher."

In a panic, hoping to improve my score, I mailed out some samples and ballots to Irv's brother Paul and his wife Shirley in Tucson, Arizona. When the final votes came in, the bake-off ended eight to five. That wasn't quite so bad.

Ron confessed to me that he won because he had added an extra teaspoonful of almond extract to his batter. Now future generations will have an improved recipe, and the old crock will never be empty.

# Glossary

| | |
|---|---|
| *ayer kichel* | light cookies |
| *bar mitzvah* | ceremony when a 13-year-old Jewish boy reaches status of a man |
| *borscht* | beet soup |
| *b'rocheh* | blessing |
| *bubbe* | grandma |
| *ca'leh* | bride |
| *challa* | braided egg bread |
| *Chanukah menorah* | candlestick with eight branches, plus a center candle, the *shamus*, which is used to light the daily candles |
| *Chanukah* | Eight-day Festival of Lights |
| *chazir* | pig |
| *Cheder* | Hebrew school |
| *cho'sen* | groom |
| *gadempta flaish* | stew |
| *ha-motsi* | bread blessing |
| *Ioykit* | sighed and grunted |
| *klatch* | a gathering |
| *knishes* | dumplings |
| *kugel* | pudding |
| *lokshen* | noodle |
| *mandel broyt* | crisp cookie |
| *matzo balls* | dumplings made from crushed matzos |
| *mazel tov* | congratulations or good luck |
| *meshugeh* | crazy |
| *minyan* | ten men required for prayer |

| | |
|---|---|
| *mitzvah* | good deed |
| *narishkite* | foolishness |
| *Oy vey* | Woe is me! |
| *pogrom* | massacre of Jews |
| *rag sheeney* | person who collects old clothes and rags |
| *schnapps* | liquor |
| *Shabbos* | Sabbath |
| *shlep* | drag |
| *shnook* | timid person |
| *shul* | synagogue |
| *shvitz* | to sweat |
| *yahrzeit* | anniversary of a loved one's death |
| *Yiddish* | language of the Jews of Eastern Europe |
| *zey gezunt* | go in good health |
| *zol zine sha it* | it should be quiet |

*"Zey Gezunt" (Go in good health)*

***Steve, Bam, and Ron, 1998*** *Steve is an electrical engineer;
Ron is an M.D. and two years from certification as an
orthopedic surgeon. Both are happily married and I have a
great-grandson, Clay. Am I a proud grandma, or what!*

# About the Author

This book is a collection of little stories compiled and written by Jean which were recalled and incorporated into her one-woman show, "Growing Up in a Jewish Home," performed for many diverse audiences. Jean was a 1967 International Toastmistress speech contest winner; in 1968 was commissioned as Ambassador of Goodwill for Colorado; received a Red Cross Award for entertaining troops, patients, and veterans and has been a guest of KOA Radio, CBS, and NBC News. When Jean placed first in all competitions to qualify for the preliminaries at the International Toastmistress Club Convention speech contest, the *Los Angeles Times* said "Jean was enjoyed equally by the young and old, male and female, happy and unhappy." She was asked by one of the judges, "if she realized she had made a thousand bitter jealous women laugh?"

Jean was a wonderful wife, is a best friend to her daughter, much revered by her grandchildren, was a marvelous sister and aunt, is a great friend to many – and most of all, a delightful person with whom to share time. Irv called her "The Golden Hands" for she could make something out of nothing, and in her presentation at Jean's 80th birthday party, her daughter said her "mom is the best cook in the U.S. and Canada, bar none. She can make pillows, drapes, quilts, dolls, miniature rooms, refinishes furniture, and fixes most things in the house that need fixing." Candy continued, "At 80 you are so young and vital because you stay interested and you are so alive and alert because you think pleasant thoughts and do good things and you have always made up your mind to make the best of any situation."

While the book is not always funny, her essence and sense of humor can be felt. Her love of people and her heritage savors the disappearing era.

# Accolades

MORTIMER I. GORDON
BGEN USAF (RET)
3673 South Elm Way
Denver, CO 80237-1010

15 MAY 78

Dear Jean,

Marianne and I have recently Returned from a week in Tarzana, Ca.

I had my first opportunity to just Relax and meditate in a long time. I brought your book "Oy Vey" with me. Once I started to read same, I could hardly put it down. At home there is scarcely enough time these days for normal chores.

Your book is most enjoyable and relaxing reading. I could not put it down because I wanted to find out what was next, next, etc.

My only disappointment came when I finished reading the book and there was no more!

Our congratulations for such a professional and interesting book. We look forward to the next book!

I would recommend your book to all who appreciate family warmth, sentimentality, family history and just good writing skill.

Your Friends,

Marianne + Mort

# DENVER PUBLIC SCHOOLS

ROBERT D. GILBERTS, Superintendent

ADMINISTRATION BUILDING • 414 FOURTEENTH STREET • DENVER, COLORADO 80202

DEPARTMENT OF GENERAL CURRICULUM SERVICES
WILLIAM R. SPEARS, Administrative Director

January 20, 1969

Jean Isaacson
1301 Hudson Street
Denver, Colorado 80202

Dear Miss Isaacson:

This letter is to confirm your acceptance to judge
at the Denver Public Schools Speech Meet to be
held at West High School, 951 Elati Street, on
Saturday, February 1, 1969.

The tournament director for the meet is Mr. Carl
Johnson who has prepared your judging assignments.
Please report to the Judge's desk prior to 8:00 a.m.
on the day of the meet to receive your assignments.

A light lunch will be served.  Coffee and doughnuts
will be provided for you throughout the day.

Sincerely,

Leonard Kramish
Coordinator, Speech
and Drama Activities

LK:vsl

# STATE OF COLORADO

## OFFICE OF THE SECRETARY OF STATE

UNITED STATES OF AMERICA,  ss.    **CERTIFICATE·**
STATE OF COLORADO.

*I, Byron A. Anderson, Secretary of State of the State of Colorado, do hereby certify that*

TO ALL TO WHOM THESE PRESENTS SHALL COME, GREETINGS:

KNOW YE THAT I,

BYRON A. ANDERSON, Secretary of State of the State of Colorado, reposing special faith and confidence in

MRS. I. J. ISAACSON

do hereby commission her AMBASSADOR OF GOOD WILL, hereby authorizing and empowering her to execute and discharge all and singular the duties appertaining to said office, and to enjoy all the privileges and immunities thereof for the term ending in happiness. . . . . . .

*IN TESTIMONY WHEREOF I have hereunto set my hand and affixed the Great Seal of the State of Colorado, at the City of Denver, this* –Twenty-second– *day of* –October– *A. D.* 1968

*Byron A. Anderson*
SECRETARY OF STATE

**VETERANS ADMINISTRATION**
WASHINGTON 25, D. C.

nov 1 1960

DEPARTMENT OF INSURANCE

YOUR FILE REFERENCE:

IN REPLY REFER TO: **933**

Mrs. Jean Isaacson
Veterans Administration Center
Denver Federal Center
Denver 2, Colorado

THROUGH: Mr. E. R. Benke, Manager

Congratulations, Mrs. Isaacson,

. . . on your selection as a three-time best letter-of-the-
month winner.

This is indeed a distinction and you have reason to be
proud of this fine achievement.

Keep up the good work!

Very truly yours,

R. T. BROWN
Acting Chief Insurance Director

r woman should, if possible, give veteran's name and file number, whether
If such number is unknown, service or serial numbers should be given.

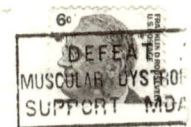

INTERNATIONAL
TOASTMISTRESS

"ITC PRESIDENT IN DENVER"

Mrs. Hillery    Mrs. Isaacson

"State Toastmistress week", proclaimed by Govenor John Love,
was celebrated October 20-26. Here to promote Toastmistress
was Viola A. Hillery, International President, whose visit
in Denver was sponsored by Northland Toastmistress Club.
She was honored at a well-attended dinner meeting at the
Tiffin Inn Tuesday evening, October 22, at which Judy McCoy
of Northland Club presided. George V. Kelly, administrative
assistant to Mayor Tom Currigan, presented the "Denver
Spoon" to Viola to enable her to "stir things up" in Toastmistress. Byron Anderson, Colorado Secretary of State,
welcomed Viola on behalf of Govenor Love and invested in her
the powers of the Secretary of State with his personal proc-
lamation.

Four members of Denver Club, Sylvia Murray, Pat Brydon,
Gertrude Martin, and Evelyn Johnston gave a humorous skit
on etiquette "To Tell the Toastmistress Member" which was
written by Joan Spahn of Denver Club. Delores Lopez of
Northland Club gave the commercials as Phyllis Diller. Jean
Isaacson delighted the audience with a composite of mono-
logue and readings entitled "A Fun Package". Toastmistress,
Francie Koehler introduced Viola as the featured speaker for
the evening who implemented her year's theme "Build a Better
World" with her talk "ITC--Architects of the Future".

Wednesday, October was proclaimed as "Toastmistress Day" in
Denver and Viola concluded her activities by appearing at
KOA-TV Channel 4 for a taped interview on the Merri Lynn
Show. The Hillery's are touring nine ITC Regions by auto
and are planning on being back in California the middle of
November so that Viola can resume her duties as Chief Assist-
and Accountant for the Department of Airports at Los Angeles
International Airport. She has the distinction of being the
only woman to hold this position in city civil service.

* 3 *

**The National Secretaries Association**

*(International)*

*Little-Wood Chapter*
ENGLEWOOD AND LITTLETON,
COLORADO

*Please reply to:*

October 30, 1968

Dear Jean:

Judging from the encore Saturday after your presentation, this letter of appreciation will probably not bring any news to you. But we do want to express our thanks for the nice windup you gave to Saturday's Workshop.

The comments about the program were very receptive for the entire presentation, and a number of people expressed that the luncheon speech was the perfect wrapup, as well as being a lot of fun.

Our thanks and good wishes to you.

Sincerely,

(Mrs.) Madelyn Nold
President

 # Air Force Academy Officers' Wives' Club

United States Air Force Academy, Colorado

October 26, 1967

Mrs. I. J. Isaacson
7310 Hudson St.
Denver, Colorado  80220

Dear Mrs. Isaacson,

On behalf of the Officers' Wives' Club I would like to thank you for a most delightful, entertaining, afternoon. I'm sure we've all become exasperated with our men...but bless them all...what would we do without them! Your clever, imaginative presentations sparked everyones sense of humor, something we should all never forget.

We all enjoyed meeting you, and sincerely wish you continued success in your career.

Very sincerely yours,

Jane Francke
(Mrs. F. W. Francke)
Corresponding Secretary

**WEIGHT WATCHERS®**

2184 SO. COLORADO BLVD./DENVER/COLORADO/TEL: (303)-756-9491

AREA NO. 71

AREA DIRECTORS
JULES GREEN
CAROL GREEN

LOCATIONS:

ARVADA
AURORA
BOULDER
BROOMFIELD
COLORADO SPRINGS
DENVER
ENGLEWOOD
ESTES PARK
FORT COLLINS
GOLDEN
GREELEY
LAKEWOOD
LITTLETON
LONGMONT
NORTHGLENN
PUEBLO
SECURITY
WESTMINSTER
WHEATRIDGE

April 21, 1971

Dear Jean,

Thank you so much for appearing with me on the radio show last week. You were such a delight - and a real bright spot in my otherwise miserable day! It was good to have some-one as capable as you. You did a **great** job - thanks again,

Sincerely,

Carol Green

May 7, 1970


Mrs. Jean B. Isaacson
1301 Hudson Street
Denver, Colorado   80220

Dear Jean:

You were certainly a hit last night!   I've seen many little buzz
groups today discussing and rediscussing your many helpful
hints and humerous remarks.   They were particularly impressed
with your changes of accessories for your basic black dress.

I particularly enjoyed the evening and talking with you about
Weight Watchers.   Although I'm not yet motivated enough to join
or to diet strictly, at least I am thinking along those lines.
Your daughter's remark to you about do you ever lose the feeling
that you're _____ (darling wasn't the word, but it will do)
particularly hit close to my motivating point.    So you tell your
daughter that if I decide to join, she'll be partially responsible.

Incidentally, here is your check and thanks again for a delightful
evening.

Cordially,

_Ruth_

Miss Ruth E. Holt
TGI Club
The Dow Chemical Company
Rocky Flats Division
P. O. Box 888
Golden, Colorado   80401


reh
Enc.

# Thank You

## Review This Book

Enjoyed *Oy Vey*? Your feedback means the world! If the book resonated with you, inspired you, or offered something meaningful, we'd truly appreciate it if you left an honest/brief review on Amazon or Goodreads. Your feedback helps others discover the book—and it directly supports the author's work.

QR

# RED THREAD BOOKS
## write · publish · impact

**About the Publisher**

Red Thread Publishing is an award-winning indie press dedicated to amplifying powerful, authentic nonfiction voices. In our first five years, we've published more than 68 books, supported over 320 authors from 30 countries, and celebrated 39 book awards, proof of the impact and quality behind every title we produce.

Our passionate team is committed to guiding authors through every step of the writing and publishing journey so their stories not only get published but make a lasting impact.

Visit **www.redthreadbooks.com**

Email us **info@redthreadbooks.com**

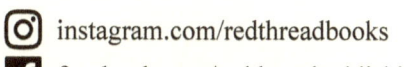 instagram.com/redthreadbooks

facebook.com/redthreadpublishing